OBACHAN

A YOUNG GIRL'S STRUGGLE FOR FREEDOM IN
TWENTIETH-CENTURY JAPAN

TANI HANES

Obachan, 1960s

*This memoir is dedicated to the memory of my obachan, my
grandma, who was one of the strongest, kindest, and most capable
women I ever knew. She knew everything there was to be known
about flowers; whenever I showed her a photograph of someone
or someplace, she would always squint and say in Japanese,
"What is that blooming right there behind him? Right there next
to the table?" She always took the tiniest slice of cake (she loved
sweets), the most overcooked piece of fish; she never felt she
deserved any more, she'd been trained this way, which made
me sad.*

*I never realized my obachan was an unhappy woman until I
asked her one evening if she loved my grandfather. She said of
course she didn't.*

I stared at her.

I asked how she could bear to be touched by him, then, and she told me matter-of-factly that she couldn't. She couldn't!

This shocked me. It had never occurred to me that she'd feel this way about him. She'd married him, after all. Don't get me wrong, I believe there was affection between them. They were married for nigh on half a century, how could there not be? But romantic love? I don't think so.

This was what led her to tell me her life story, in bits and pieces, whenever my baby was asleep, or as we'd sip iced tea at my house in California. And that was when I realized that I never really knew her at all, and the clock was ticking if I wanted to change that.

So here's my attempt. I hope, wherever she is, she's pleased with it. And that she's surrounded by flowers and noshing on the biggest piece of cake.

She sure as hell deserves it.

1

AN UNGRATEFUL GIRL

The only known photograph of the entire Ishikawa family together: Mitsuko's mother on the far left, Mitsuko's father next to her, brothers, sisters and their children in between, and Mitsuko on the far right, ca 1936.

The full moon shone down on the sleeping village. It was sinking in the west, illuminating many square *ri* of rice fields, filled with top-heavy stalks of ready-to-be-harvested rice. Walkways divided the paddies into symmetrical shapes, framing the fronds into rustling squares.

Twelve-year-old Mitsuko lay on the pallet that she shared with two of her younger sisters, twisting and turning as she tried to sleep. Her back was sore from a day spent tending the rice, and she counted the days until the harvest would be over and she could return to school. It was the autumn of 1928, and she had missed nearly a full month already.

Suddenly a candle was thrust in her face, and she heard her mother's voice.

"Good, you're still awake. Come in the other room. Your father and I want to talk to you."

She got out of bed without a word and threaded her way between the sleeping bodies of her brothers and sisters.

Her father was sitting on the only chair, so she stood in front of him, while her mother, still holding the candle, went to stand behind. He cleared his throat.

"You know that the harvest this year won't be very good."

Mitsuko nodded. The harvest was never good; it was too warm. Niigata, which was a three-day ride to the north, was where the high-quality rice was produced.

"You are young and fat," he said. Everyone knew that fat people didn't get sick as often. "Your aunt and uncle have no children, and they have agreed to adopt you and make you their heir. They will teach you how to run their farm, and someday, you will inherit it." He leaned back, signaling that he was finished speaking.

Her mother spoke now, leaning forward and making the candle flicker. The flame danced and stretched, sending up wispy curls of smoke. "You've always been a lucky child. You survived the malaria that killed your older sister, and you're so sturdy."

Mitsuko stared at the candle as the flame guttered dangerously. She thought of the school where she went, the school that was an hour's walk from her house. Her aunt and uncle lived half a day's journey in the opposite direction.

"They won't be coming for you until early next year, because we'll need you through the worst of the winter," her mother continued. A dollop of wax fell with a hiss to the floor. "Work hard for them, and don't make us ashamed of you."

The candle flame guttered for the final time and burned out.

MITSUKO FIDGETED with the front of her *hanten*, the heavy winter garment she'd tied over her least worn kimono. She wiped the steam off the window facing the road, trying to see if more snow had fallen during the night. Although it was March, spring was still two weeks away, and if there was fresh snow, her only good shoes would be soaked by the time she reached the school.

She was startled by her sister Hanako's voice. She'd thought that she was the only one awake.

"You know that Ma won't let you go to school," she said from the pallet they shared. "Aunt and Uncle are coming to get you."

Mitsuko only nodded.

"Didn't you tell your teacher that you wouldn't be able to come today, that you wouldn't be able to give the graduation speech?"

Mitsuko shook her head, biting her lip.

"Well, if you're going to go, you'd better get going now, before she wakes up."

As Mitsuko opened the door, her sister said, "If she asks me where you went, I'll just tell her that I don't know."

Mitsuko flashed a grateful smile and stepped outside.

The day was bright already, and fiercely cold. The air was so clear that she felt she could reach out and touch Mount Fuji, though it was a two-day ride to the southeast. It rose sharply from the plains, dusted in white from top to bottom, contrasting sharply with the dark blue sky.

She hurried along the road, blowing on her fingers to keep them warm. Her breath came out in smoke-like puffs, like the plow horses in the Hayashi's field when they were working hard.

She came to the bridge that spanned Kawara Creek and crossed it quickly, not taking time as she usually did to stop and watch the water as it wound its way beneath her. Mount Fuji was the only thing in her field of vision that hadn't changed position since she'd left her house.

She heard the far-off whistle of the train and, even more faintly, the clicking of its wheels against the steel rails on which it rode. That had to be the morning freight, which meant that it was already after eight o'clock. She quickened her brisk step, thinking of her speech, of how proud she'd been when selected to give it. She smiled to herself.

The smell of cooking fish reached her, a smoky, salty smell, reminding her that she hadn't had any breakfast, and only rice for dinner the night before. She tried to take her mind off it, but her disloyal stomach began to growl and, finally, to cramp from hunger.

She bent down and scooped up some snow in her chapped hands. It felt soft, like the finely shaved ice that she'd been lucky enough to eat one summer, although that ice had had strawberry syrup on it. She packed it with her two hands into roughly the shape of a rice ball, and felt it harden, losing its velvety texture and becoming like a piece of the lava she sometimes found in the field. She took a bite. It tasted like the outdoors, like the wind that whipped around her ankles. She chewed on it, enjoying the squeaky texture of the snow against the flat of her back molars. The minerals in the snow left a tingling on her tongue, and she swallowed it and took another bite. She resumed walking, periodically taking bites of her snowball.

She passed more people as she neared the town, and they said, "Good morning," as they bobbed their heads. She bobbed her head in return with her own murmured greeting.

Suddenly she heard a dog begin to bark, quite close by, the quick volleys of barking that indicate that they've found something exciting. He burst out onto the road right in front of her, chasing something small. He chased it into the drainage ditch that ran alongside the road, then stood at bay, barking with delight. She looked into the ditch, which was frozen over in a milky gray color. She bent down and looked off near the end, where a grate covered the underground opening, and at first she could only see the brightly colored bits of garbage that had been trapped there. Then something moved, and she saw that it was a rabbit, pushing itself up against the grate, turning to fight whatever was chasing it. It was wild with fright, and utterly trapped. It had nowhere to go.

She contemplated the rabbit for a moment, wondering if the dog would give up and leave. But the dog continued to bark and began to close in.

Mitsuko straightened up and continued on her way, turning around from time to time to see if the dog had moved. When she came to a bend in the road, she turned for one last look. The dog was still there.

She quickened her steps as she finished walking to school, trying to keep warm, and hoped someone had unlocked the building so she could get inside. She tugged on the door and found that it slid easily, so she let herself in and closed it behind her quickly, trying not to let the warmth from the stove out.

She fumbled with the strings that held her hanten closed and looked around to see if anyone else had arrived at the schoolhouse yet. It was still dark inside, and she could barely make out the scroll hanging on one wall, where every graduate's name had been written in beautiful *oshuji*, the traditional Japanese calligraphy, by her teacher. She looked reverently at the bold brush strokes, hanging in the darkened room, and saw her own name, "Ishikawa, Mitsuko," at the very top, in the place of honor.

She could feel herself relaxing here, in this peaceful place of learning, where so many of her happiest memories had been made. It didn't matter to her that she had to bring her younger brothers and sisters with her to play under her desk; she was happy to do it, happy to do anything that would let her sit with the other students and *learn*, acquire *knowledge* of the big world that lay beyond this tiny village where she lived.

She was still staring at the scroll when she heard the clatter of the door being slid open behind her. She turned to see who it was.

It was her mother.

She looked at Mitsuko with her lips pursed, her slight, stooped form tight with anger, like a tiger ready to spring.

"What do you think you're doing?" Her mother brandished her fist. "What kind of bad, ungrateful girl are you?" She took a step closer, but it was still difficult to see her in the gloom of the schoolhouse. Mitsuko first thought that her mother looked like one of the demons that were supposed to haunt the local temple, indistinct but grotesquely terrifying. Then, as she looked closer, she realized that she was looking at her own face, marked by the passage of the hard years, features pressed to stone by fate.

"They're on their way to get you, they left last night." Her mother's face contorted with rage, her mouth twisting. Mitsuko could see the fine spray of spit as it flew from her mother's mouth. "They're probably at the house now. What are they going to think? They're going to think that you don't want to go! How could you be so ungrateful? You've shamed us all."

She turned to go back outside.

"Come."

Mitsuko stayed where she was.

Her mother turned around. "Come. We might be able to catch them. Just because you're too much of a fool to see how fortunate you are, you're not going to ruin it for everyone."

Mitsuko shook her head.

"Stupid girl! Idiot! What do you think you're going to get here?" Her mother waved her gnarled hand around to encompass the schoolhouse. "You think you can eat the words they teach you to write? You think the paper is going to turn into a bowl of rice? You think you can wear the words you learn to read? That they'll keep you warm in winter?"

She strode to where Mitsuko stood and raised her hand.

Mitsuko flinched, expecting a blow, but instead she felt her hair being ripped out of her head. Her mother gave a vicious yank, and the two of them stumbled out into the morning, her mother hanging on to her hair.

"No!" Mitsuko felt the word being torn from the bottom of her soul. "No! No! NO!" She began to cry as her mother pulled her down the street by her hair. People turned from their various morning chores, sweeping their porches and opening up their shops, to stare. Her mother looked straight in front of her, walking out of the village, pulling her daughter behind her.

Mitsuko was walking bent at the waist, both hands clasped around her mother's skinny wrist, begging, crying. She saw the people staring as they passed.

She saw some people waiting to buy things from the tobacconist's, which was just opening. One of the people looked very familiar; she'd seen that elegant topcoat somewhere before. Then he began to turn, and she realized that he was her teacher. He held a newspaper in his hand. She remembered that he was one of a handful of people in the village who could read the entire newspaper. She saw him turn, saw him see her. She closed her eyes and was silent. Her hot, shameful tears dripped from her face, and she finally let go of her mother's hands to wipe them and cover her face, so she wouldn't have to see him, see the pity in his intelligent eyes.

She stumbled and nearly fell, kept from doing so only by the iron grip of her mother on her hair. Her best kimono ripped, a defeated sound. She opened her eyes when she was sure that she would no longer see her teacher, and saw she was filthy, muddied from the waist down.

Her mother didn't let go of her hair until they reached the house.

"They've gone," her father announced from the doorway when they arrived.

Mitsuko tried to go around him, but he reached for her as she passed and pushed her down into the dirt. "Your aunt and uncle were so disappointed. They say that they no longer want to adopt you. I will see what I can do to change their minds. We will not speak of this again." He looked down at her. "I am so ashamed," he added, turning and entering the house.

Mitsuko lay quite still until she was sure her father wasn't coming back. Then she rose, slowly, pushing herself up from the dirt, tucking her hair behind her ear as she stood. She brushed the dust from the torn kimono and turned to see her brothers and sisters watching her from the windows and doorway, eyes wide, completely silent.

She walked slowly toward the house, dropping her ruined clothing just inside the door and taking the replacements her sister held out to her.

"Thank you," she murmured, shouldering on the threadbare but clean shirt and pulling on the pants.

"Auntie and Uncle were really upset," her sister whispered.

Mitsuko just nodded, hurrying to do her chores. What she really wanted to do was go back to school and see if she was in time to give the speech. She wasn't going back to her aunt and uncle's farm, after all; why not try to salvage one good thing from this horrible, ruined day? But she didn't ask, knowing all it would gain her was probably a beating.

The rest of the day passed, then the next, with no more mention being made of her going to the farm, and Mitsuko began to think maybe this awful idea had been shelved.

The last thing she wanted was to be heir to their horrible "farm," their bare patch of dirt where hardly anything would grow, where hours and days and months of toil barely yielded enough to provide sustenance for *them*, let alone anything worth selling to others. Living on their farm would likely do nothing but put her dreams of going to school even farther out of her reach.

Eventually, the bitter, harsh winter ended as spring came to their remote corner of Japan, and Mitsuko's father got their cart out of the ramshackle barn, checking the wheels and frame for soundness, and sent his son to the neighbor's to see if their mule could be borrowed for the day.

Mitsuko, her sisters, and her mother woke up early and

made *onigiri*, rice balls, for everyone, which they carefully wrapped in cloth and packed in baskets in the bottom of the cart before covering them with blankets so they wouldn't get dusty. Then, the whole family climbed in, the older children holding the younger ones, and set off.

The cart rattled as it bounced over the unpaved road, swaying like a small ship. Mitsuko looked around her, at the spring that had finally come. The countryside was dotted with splashes of pink and white from the various trees that were in bloom. A huge *sakura* waved its branches in the breeze, and the cart and its occupants were showered in the pink petals of cherry blossoms when they passed underneath.

It was their annual trip to the mountains to look for sedge grass with which to make shoes. The entire family went. On the way up, they were allowed to ride, but on the way back, they would have to walk, as the cart would be piled with sedge grass. Everyone would get a new pair of shoes, then her father would take the extras to town to try to sell them. Mitsuko rocked her baby brother in her arms, singing a tuneless melody to soothe him. When they reached the hillside, everyone got out of the cart and began to pick. The greenest grass, which made the tightest, most waterproof shoes, was the hardest to pull, and Mitsuko's hands were soon stained green from it. Every time the carrier on her back was full, she would go back to the cart and toss it over her head with an experienced heave.

There was a lark singing nearby, and cicadas droned tunelessly in the trees. Hanako smiled at her and gestured for Mitsuko to follow. Mitsuko followed her sister behind a stand of poplars and smiled when she saw what Hanako had found. She reached out her hand, picked a blackberry, put it in her mouth, and turned to her sister. It was early for them; they were lucky. She showed her teeth in a purple grin, and both girls picked and ate in silence for five minutes.

"Hanako!" They heard their father's voice from the other side of the poplars. "Hanako! Come here!"

Hanako turned to Mitsuko and grimaced. "Be right back." And she was gone.

Mitsuko stayed for a few more minutes, waiting for Hanako and eating blackberries. The day had become hot and oppressive, the thick air wrapping around her and squeezing the sweat out of her pores. She heard a sound behind her and turned, expecting to see her sister, but it was just a rabbit. It bounded off into the brush.

Reluctantly, Mitsuko turned back toward the cart. She brushed her purple stained hands against some tree trunks to try to remove the color. She stopped at a little stream, got a drink, and washed her hands thoroughly.

She stepped into the clearing where the cart had been, but only the tracks it had made in the grass remained. Mitsuko carefully searched for her brothers and sisters, and looked down the road to see if her father had moved the cart. She called out, but only the lark answered her.

She heard the rattle of different wheels coming up the road, and ran towards it, but she stopped when it came into view. The cart was much smaller than the one she'd ridden up in. Her aunt and uncle sat silently inside. They pulled it to a stop in front of her, but she just stood for a moment, looking at the ground.

Mitsuko finally looked up one last time, hoping against hope that her parents hadn't done this to her, hadn't brought her up here and simply *abandoned* her to her aunt and uncle without even telling her they were going to do it.

But it seemed they had, for they, and her brothers and sisters, were nowhere to be found.

Her uncle jiggled the reins impatiently. Mitsuko bit back her tears, knowing they'd do her no good, and grabbed the old, splintery wood frame of the cart to swing herself aboard. She took her partially filled sedge grass carrier off of her back and set it down next to her feet. Her uncle clucked at the mule, and it began plodding slowly toward their house.

2

FARMER GIRL

Mitsuko woke up when the sun was high enough over the horizon to shine into her eyes through the bare window. Her Uncle Kazuo and Aunt Sachi were lucky enough to have actual glass in their windows, but they had no money, nor indeed any inclination for such niceties as curtains. Why would a person want curtains? If the sun is up, you should be up anyway, and outside, working.

She rose from her pallet and stepped outside to haul the water for their morning wash, and their tea and rice. A blast of cold air and dirt blew in before she could get the door closed, and she knew that the dirt just inside would get tracked all over unless she remembered to sweep it back outside before her aunt and uncle rose.

The birds were awake and singing, birds that sounded somehow different here in northern Fukushima prefecture. She kept her eyes grimly focused on the ground in front of her. Why should she look around at the trees, or the grass, or worse, the road that ran past the farm?

All represented freedom, escape, things she didn't have access to.

She tucked her sleeves into the *obi* tied around her waist as she hauled the water up from the well and dumped it into buckets, which she then hoisted, one in each hand, to walk back across the yard to the house. Behind the main building, she could see the fields, neatly tilled and partially planted with this year's potato crop.

Mitsuko hated potatoes.

She went back in the house and began her morning chores, her indoor chores to be completed before her aunt and uncle woke up. As soon as the water boiled, she woke up her aunt and began to assemble their sparse breakfast.

Shortly after, her uncle was awake and ready to wash up, and within fifteen minutes, all three of them were headed outside to finish planting the fields.

Mitsuko grabbed her bag of potato chunks and bent over the first row, ignoring the spike of pain that buried itself in her back almost immediately. She'd been doing this for weeks, her body should've adjusted to this posture already, shouldn't it? Her fingers soon grew numb from working the cold soil, and she watched them as if they belonged to someone else as they pushed the pieces into the earth and covered them over.

The sun rose higher as she moved down the row, and she tried to time her work so she'd be close to the road when the girls rode by. Today she was lucky, and they came whizzing by, chattering, laughing, bells on their bicycles ringing merrily as they called back and forth to each other. "Tomo-chan! Do you want to stop at the sweet shop after school?" one girl called to another. Her school uniform, a sailor outfit, complete with a jaunty cap, fluttered in the breeze she created as she pedaled.

"Yes, let's!" her friend responded with a smile. The group of girls passed Mitsuko as she bent to her task, oblivious to her presence.

Mitsuko rose to a standing position briefly, shading her eyes to watch as they rode out of sight. Their shiny, black backpacks shone in the morning sun as they headed into the nearby village for a day spent reading, writing, learning.

Mitsuko adjusted her clothes and bent again to her work, this time watching as her tears mixed with what came out of her running nose and dripped off the tip of it. In this way she watered the year's crop of potatoes at her aunt and uncle's farm, and she knew she'd never be able to eat one without tasting her own bitterness.

They took a short break for lunch and sat in the shade provided by the house to eat their rice. Mitsuko knew they were lucky to have rice to eat; this was a potato farm, and normally a person ate what the farm provided. Her aunt and uncle were too impoverished to buy the "new rice" that became available in the fall, but they did have access to regular rice for most of the year, until it ran out, usually in late summer.

"You're still almost as fat as when you came," her uncle remarked to her. "I guess you like living here."

"Living here is fine," Mitsuko agreed.

"That's one of the reasons we wanted you," her aunt told her. "We considered your younger sister, but we knew she'd already been sick once, and she's so skinny. You're like a nice, white pig, aren't you?" She smiled at Mitsuko, sun-weathered cheeks rising, making her eyes nearly disappear.

Mitsuko nodded, smiling back. She knew she was lucky, lucky to be so fat and healthy, lucky to still have all of her own teeth, lucky to have never been sick, lucky to have been adopted by her aunt and uncle, who were kind to her and had a farm to offer...

She couldn't help thinking of the girls, who were her age, whose hands were unmarked by toil and strife, who got to put on clean uniforms and ride their bicycles to school every day, laughing about the sweet shop.

Jealousy burned inside her; she couldn't help it.

Someday, she would go back to school.

Lunch was over quickly, and she returned to the fields, her sack of potato chunks slung over her shoulder. Her mind wandered as she continued with her work.

Someday she would have a small house that she lived in alone. In this house, she would have a little, square table. It would belong just to her, and no one else. She would keep a vase filled with flowers on the table, which would sit in front of a window that could be seen from the street. She would own the vase, and the window, and the view. In the closet would be bedding for one person, but double the width, that she didn't have to share with anyone. A fluffy, white, new futon set. Clean. Not a pallet. Just for her. And there would be only one chair at the table, for her to sit in, whenever she wanted. She wouldn't have to step around people, ever.

Someday.

3

LIFE ON THE FARM

Mitsuko first became aware of the field rabbit on a hot, late-spring day when she was, of course, out planting. She was wearing as little clothing as she could while still remaining decent, and she had a rag tied over her mouth and nose to avoid breathing in the dirt as much as possible. It was miserably hot and humid already. There were three dark spots on the rag on her face, two small ones for her nostrils, and one large one for her mouth, where the dirt had stuck to the rag. She'd laughed when she saw her reflection in the creek at her lunch break the first day she wore the rag, for she looked like a pig, her mouth open in perpetual surprise.

She came across the rabbit hole in the last planting row, the row closest to the creek, a small opening in the soil that slanted down toward the water. She knew what she was supposed to do. She was supposed to fill in the hole with soil and rocks and salt, then pour water over the entire thing, and if that didn't work, she was supposed to wait in the early morning next to the hole with a large stone in her hand, and kill the rabbit when it came out to feed.

But on the first day that she saw it, she was hungry, and it was close to lunch, and all she did was mark the spot, and promise herself to come back and do the job the next day.

The next day, however, it was raining, a horrible, warm, heavy rain; she just wanted to finish her work and get out of the wet and mosquitoes, and of course they were worst near the creek, so she left it.

The next time she remembered and went to the spot with the shovel, she was surprised by the rabbit herself, peeking out of the hole, even though it was still late afternoon, and neither early morning nor evening when the small rodents liked to come out and perform their mischief.

Mitsuko stood up straight with shock and saw her aunt's short form taking in the laundry from the line close to the house. She waved at Mitsuko and made brisk shoveling motions, turning the fake shovel over to mimic filling in the hole.

Are you getting the job done?

Mitsuko nodded reassuringly and smiled, adding a wave in case her aunt couldn't see the smile because of the distance.

She looked down and the small, brown creature was gone, but even as she looked, the rabbit's face appeared once again in the hole, black eyes bright and shining, whiskers twitching, and Mitsuko was enchanted. Her smile remained where it was, and she spoke to the rabbit, causing her long, translucent ears to twitch in Mitsuko's direction.

"Hey, you little troublemaker, what are you doing out at this time of day? It's so hot, shouldn't you be sleeping down in your nice, cool house?"

Mitsuko could smell the rabbit, an earthy, gamey smell, and wondered if the animal could smell her as well. She was astounded at its apparent and complete lack of fear. The rabbit disappeared back into her burrow for a moment, and Mitsuko watched the dark opening, hopeful that she'd return.

Sure enough, within a few seconds, she was back, eyes like liquid seeming to look up at her.

"I don't have anything for the likes of you," Mitsuko told the rabbit. "You should run and hide from me, don't you know that? Don't you know what this is?" She raised the shovel. "I'm here to cave in the front of your house, you silly animal."

The rabbit merely twitched her gossamer whiskers in Mitsuko's direction, almost as if she could understand her but was laughing at what she was saying.

"Can you understand me? Do you understand my words?" Mitsuko spoke in a soft lilt to the rabbit.

"Mitsuko? Hurry up! It's time to eat, and I still need you to bring the water up!" her aunt called from the house.

"Yes, I'm sorry, I'm coming!" Mitsuko responded. She turned toward the house without doing a thing to the burrow and without a backward glance.

"Did you take care of the varmint?" her uncle asked when she returned to the house.

Mitsuko nodded as she put the shovel away.

"Rabbits are terrible pests," he continued as he took the rice his wife passed him, bowing his thanks. "Even a small warren of rabbits can ruin an entire field of potatoes, you know, never mind a garden."

Mitsuko wondered about calling their pitiful attempt at vegetables a "garden," but only nodded again as she ate her pickles and rice.

After dinner, as she was putting her dishes away, she deftly grabbed some cabbage leaf cuttings out of the raw garbage bag on the counter and put it in her pocket when no one was looking. Then she picked up the buckets and told her aunt she was going to the creek for the water.

"Thank you, Mitsuko. You're such a good girl, such a help to us," her aunt responded with a nod.

When she got to the bank, she set the buckets down and spread the cabbage leaves out in front of the rabbit hole, smiling to herself.

OVER THE NEXT FEW DAYS, Mitsuko would leave a few scraps around the mouth of the rabbit's burrow whenever she could. It was never very much, because they were a very thrifty household, and there was never much to spare. Carrots were eaten with the peel on, bug holes on leafy greens were simply carefully ripped out; the entire leaf was rarely thrown away.

But Mitsuko did what she could, and soon the rabbit, whom she simply called *Usagi-san*, Ms. Rabbit, would poke her head out of her burrow whenever she felt Mitsuko's footfalls above her. Mitsuko wondered if the rabbit actually recognized her footsteps and could distinguish them from her aunt's and uncle's. But they rarely worked this end of the field; it was the farthest from the house, and they left it to their young niece.

Once or twice, Mitsuko even woke up extra early, when the dawn was just a misty blue in the east, and walked out to the burrow with a piece of turnip in her pocket, just to see *Usagi-san* and talk to her.

She got such a thrill to see the delicate ears, bright eyes and briskly wiggling whiskers poking out of the little hole to greet her!

Mitsuko would toss her the morsel of food and wait as

the animal slowly crept out, hopping slowly closer and closer to where it lay in the dirt. Then, she would pick it up, and to Mitsuko's surprise and joy, instead of running back to her burrow with it, she would stay outside to enjoy her snack in Mitsuko's company and remain to listen to her talk.

Mitsuko told her about how hard life on the farm was, how she didn't have any friends, how there was no chance to learn, how she missed her sister.

Usagi-san was a very sympathetic listener.

ONE MORNING, Mitsuko woke up early and grabbed a few wilted lettuce leaves from the garbage for *Usagi-san*, hurrying to get out there so she could enjoy the cool temperatures before the sun rose and everything got humid and sticky.

She was surprised to see her uncle heading toward the house, shovel over his shoulder, carrying something that dangled from his hand, something limp and dripping.

"Look! I caught a rabbit over by the river!" her uncle said, his voice pleased and excited. "We'll have fresh meat for dinner tonight!"

Mitsuko nodded and reached for the rabbit with a trembling hand.

4

THE LONG WALK HOME

They were just about finished with the potatoes and would begin planting the other vegetables soon: eggplants, carrots, and *daikon*, the large, white radishes that were common to Japan. Mitsuko closed her eyes, trying to ignore the image of the rows of dirt that seemed permanently imprinted on her eyelids. She was sick of dirt, of grit in her clothes, her hair, on her skin, in her rice, her tea—it was everywhere.

She rolled over on her pallet, looking up at the patch of night sky she could see through the window. Her exhausted aunt and uncle snored inches away from where she lay, but she closed her ears to the unpleasant sounds, imagining instead the sounds of a *vi-o-lin*, which she'd been lucky enough to hear once at the train station when she went on a field trip with her school. It was an amazing sound, the sound she imagined a bird's wings made when it flew high up in the sky, so high it was almost not visible anymore, soaring up among the clouds. It still brought tears to her eyes to remember the sounds the young man had produced with the curved, scrolled instrument and the long stick he ran over the strings.

How was it possible to live in a world that could include *that*, produce *that*, and also include vile, odious, brown *dirt*? A world that included flowers and calligraphy and books and knowledge, and also men like her father, who wanted to own you, or others, who stared at you and wanted to do worse? A world that included chocolate and vanilla, both of which she'd tasted once before in her life, and also included horrible, awful, pickled beets, surely the worst-tasting food in the world?

Through the window, Mitsuko could see the constellation Cygnus, the swan, its neck stretching out across the horizon, and she knew that the sun would be rising soon. She sighed and decided it wasn't worth trying to go back to sleep. She rose and began her morning chores.

"JUST THINK, Mitsuko, someday you'll own this farm, this land will be yours," her uncle enthused that evening. They had finished washing up and were sitting outside in the dirt, enjoying the relative cool after the sun went down.

She nodded, trying to look enthusiastic. Luckily, she was known for being a girl of few words, and no one thought it strange that she didn't say anything. Everything she could see was brown, from the earth, to the fence, the small house, outbuildings, even her flesh and clothes had all blended to the same dun color.

She didn't voice her thoughts, even to herself, but she knew what was in her head when she dumped the evening meal of pickled beets and rice into her freshly washed towel and tucked it into her shirt. She was aware of it, all night long, as they cleaned up the yard by the light of the friendly full moon.

They were all on their pallets early, as was their custom. Mitsuko went to bed in her clothes that night, which wasn't usual, but no one questioned her choice. Her aunt and uncle frequently did this, as it saved a few minutes in the morning, and the truth was that they were going to be doing the same, dirty work tomorrow as they had today, so why bother to change?

Within minutes both of her very kind relatives were snoring away, and Mitsuko rose, wincing at the creaks of her pallet. She felt bad, but she couldn't do this for one more day, she just couldn't. She slipped out the door like a shadow and was on her way.

There was only one main road in Fukushima Prefecture, and it ran right by her aunt and uncle's farm, continuing straight on for half a day's ride until it passed her mother and father's house farther south. Mitsuko set off at a brisk walk, feeling better than she had in a long time.

It was still early summer, and therefore not too hot, but the mosquitos were already out, and for most of the night Mitsuko followed the road as it ran parallel to the Akubuma River, so she got plenty of bites. It was a beautiful night, nonetheless, and Mitsuko even smiled and waved at the full moon as he shone down on her while she walked. She could hear crickets and frogs as their songs filled the night, along with myriad sounds of thousands of other night time bugs and the creatures that fed on them.

Mount Fuji, her ever-present companion, glowed off to the southwest, still with a dusting of snow, on this bright, moonlit night. Mitsuko waved to it as well, unable to quell the feeling of jubilation that welled within her. Even though she didn't know what lay ahead, she knew that she was, at least temporarily, leaving the dull world of dirty potato farming behind her. She raised her voice in song, at first tentatively, then a little louder, with a little more confidence, as she realized that no one was around for miles in the deserted Japanese countryside. Frogs and crickets alike were silenced by her renditions of numerous folk songs, but she didn't care. She sang to Fuji-san and Otsuki-san, Mount Fuji and the moon, who listened and seemed to approve.

The miles melted away under her grass shoes, brand new a few short weeks ago, already worn away to nearly flat under her sturdy feet. She passed the spot where she'd picked the very grass her father had used to make these shoes, the place where she'd been abandoned by her family earlier that year, to be picked up by her aunt and uncle and taken to their house to live.

After she'd sung a few songs, Mitsuko even began incorporating movements into her performance, throwing her arms out as she sang the loud parts, as she'd seen performers do in the village sometimes. After she finished, she listened to the night silence for a few beats. Into the stillness a bullfrog let out a single, questioning croak, as if asking what on earth that was, and Mitsuko laughed out loud, surprising herself with the sound.

When the moon was at its highest point, she unwrapped her rice and ate it, tossing the detested pickled beets away. She heard them splash into the river and smiled. As she walked along, she reflected that, even though the darkness of nighttime was supposed to be the quiet time, it was anything but. The countryside was full of scurryings, the comings and goings of animals that trod the earth and flew in the air; it was just the complementary creatures to those she knew, the ones who lived side by side with humans.

Mitsuko saw numerous rats hurrying along the road,

and even a couple of badgers trundling along, busy going wherever it was that badgers went when they weren't getting into mischief in Japanese folktales.

Finally, after she felt like she'd been walking for days, the landscape began to look familiar. Mitsuko walked to the edge of the Murakamis' field to pet their horse, Kuro, who nickered a greeting to her and trotted over, tail high.

And as the sun rose over the horizon, she let herself into her childhood home, which looked exactly the same as when she'd left it a few short weeks before. As usual, Hanako, the light sleeper, was awake, smiling at her sister from her pallet. She gestured to Mitsuko, who picked her way among her sleeping family to lie down next to her.

"You're finally home," Hanako said, smiling.

"Yes, I didn't like it up at that farm," Mitsuko replied.

Hanako nodded. "Were they nice to you?"

Mitsuko nodded, closing her eyes.

"You're going to get in trouble," Hanako said softly.

Mitsuko nodded again.

"*Okaeri, nēsan*, welcome home, big sister."

But she was already asleep.

5

SUMMERTIME

(Left to right) Hanako and Mitsuko, ca 1930

Mitsuko woke up to the sound of a chair scraping against the floor. She squinted against the light shining in her eyes, trying to shield them with her hand. She rose from the pallet, unsure what awaited her.

The room where she slept was empty, all of the pallets neatly stowed against the wall. The one she'd been sleeping on was alone, obvious in its isolation, like a stone in the middle of a clear pond. She laid the pallet next to the others and went into the next room to meet her fate.

Her father sat, his breakfast dishes on the table in front

of him. He didn't look over at her, though he must have heard her clear her pallet; he surely knew she was awake. She quaked, looking at his expression, or lack thereof, and moved forward to what awaited her.

He rose as she neared the table, and for a moment she thought he would just walk by her. She saw that her mother and one of her brothers had appeared in the doorway to the kitchen area and were hovering, looking down but remaining where they could see and hear.

Mitsuko stopped moving as her father neared, then suddenly found herself on the floor, looking at the legs of their table. She had no idea what had happened. Then she heard the sound of a slap, like an echo, in her head, and felt the immense pain in her cheek and neck. She stayed where she was, unmoving, until she was sure he was gone, then she rose, straightening one arm at a time, bracing herself, making sure her legs would bear her weight.

Wordlessly, her brother came to her side, lifting her, helping balance her until he knew she could stand. He released her as soon as he knew she was okay, leaving her in the middle of the room. Her mother came and handed her something. Mitsuko stared at it, sitting in the middle of her palm.

It was one of her molars.

It sat in her palm, small, bloody, and yellowed, bits of tissue from her mouth clinging to the roots. Luckily, it was one of the back ones, destined to fall out soon, anyway.

MITSUKO WAS ALLOWED to remain at home, and she even managed to go to school. She had her baby brother on her back and her little sister, who was three, under her desk, but she managed. She slipped her little bits of paper, folded into fun shapes, to keep her entertained. She ignored the dark looks she got from her mother when she set off for the school in the morning, and her mother let her go. As long as she minded the little ones, it would be allowed.

As the days passed, Mitsuko slowly relaxed, as much as she could. They weren't sending her back, it seemed. Nothing was said about it, at any rate. She even had some free days, when neither school nor maid work at numerous households in the village kept her away, and she was actually able to spend time with her family and just be.

She sat in the doorway of her house on such a day and watched her younger brothers and sisters gambol in the dirt yard, chasing sticks, laughing and running around. Hanako squatted next to her, chatting to her about nothing at all. It was a hot day, and summer was just around the corner.

The *omawarisan*, or neighborhood patrol officer, would sometimes stop by on his rounds, just to visit and see how things were going. It was a little unusual, since they lived so far out in the country, but also very kind of him. He was young and looked very clean, always, and freshly scrubbed. Mitsuko wondered if he was interested in Hanako, and worried. She was only twelve, after all, just a child.

As the summer wore on, the omawarisan, whose last name was Murata, came by more and more often, calling out a greeting from the street as he removed his hat and stepped into their littered yard. Mitsuko didn't like it, but she couldn't think of a way to keep him away.

She spent her days minding her siblings, cleaning houses in the village, and dreaming of a way out of her life. School was out for the brief summer holiday, and she reflected that she was probably one of the very few pupils who was sad not to be there. She knew the others made fun of her clothes, her accent, and the fact that she was babysitting while she was there.

She didn't care. It was a relief to her to be within four walls that didn't contain her father and his temper, her mother and her silent disapproval. She loved looking at the books on the shelves, knowing that they contained knowledge, worlds beyond her ken.

One day, when she was sitting in her dooryard, feeling the sun on her face, the close, humid air of summer all around her, she was surprised by Murata-san's voice, nearly in her ear. He usually stayed on the other side of the yard, talking to her brothers, giving her a polite bow before he excused himself.

"Please accept this," he murmured, bowing.

She could see his neat, black trousers, with the crease running right down the center, in front of her where she sat. His hand, which looked amazingly clean and pink to her, was right in front of her face, with the nails neat and trimmed, holding a creamy rectangle.

A letter? For her?

Hanako, who was next to her, as usual, nudged her. "*Nēsan!* Hurry up, accept it!" she urged.

Unwillingly, Mitsuko reached for it, ashamed of how large, how dirty her own hand looked. She looked up at Murata-san, who stood, so clean he practically looked like he'd been boiled, staring down at her.

She nodded her acknowledgement, unsure what to say. "I'll read it later," she finally announced, using polite honorifics.

Murata-san stood in front of her a moment longer, then nodded and bowed, tipping his hat to her as he left.

As soon as he was out of the yard, Mitsuko opened the letter, admiring the nice brushwork. He'd had some schooling, then. And he used lots of kanji, which not only meant that he was smart, but that he knew she was, too.

Next to her, Hanako, who didn't read nearly as well as she did, was bothering her, asking her what it said.

Mitsuko quickly scanned it. "Nothing," she told her sister. "Just something about the weather, and some confusing things about clouds and flowers." She stared at it a little closer. "Maybe I'm reading it backwards? Maybe he wrote it left to right, in the Western style? None of this makes any sense." She read some of it out loud.

Hanako laughed, slapping at Mitsuko's arm. "It's a poem! Nēsan, he wrote you a poem! He likes you! This is an admirer's letter!"

"It is not!" Mitsuko retorted, unable to hide her smile. "Why would he write me a letter like that?"

"He likes you!" Hanako repeated, continuing to laugh.

"Keep your voice down," Mitsuko implored, laughing. She didn't want her other brothers and sisters, or worse, her mother, to hear. And it wasn't that she was worried she'd be teased or anything; they just didn't have that kind of relationship. She felt that it wouldn't do to reveal too much of herself to her.

Meanwhile, Hanako was examining the letter very closely, even going so far as to smell it. "Nēsan, this is so beautiful, isn't it? Don't you think?" She patted Mitsuko's arm for emphasis. "His writing is so elegant. And this paper! He must have bought it in a shop, not from the monger on the street."

Mitsuko listened to her sister with half an ear, watching her little brothers and sisters playing with an old hoop in the yard, throwing stones into it as it lay in the dirt. She tried to imagine how this life, her life, looked to the nice policeman from the village.

She sighed and rose.

"Mitsuko-nēsan, where are you going?" Hanako asked.

"I have to wash some more clothes," she replied. "It's so hot, the ones from this morning are dry already, didn't you notice?" She opened the door to the house. "Watch them for me, okay?" She nodded toward the little ones in the yard.

Mitsuko gathered the dirty clothes and soiled diapers, hoisting the bag on her back as she followed the path to the river. The cicadas were very loud, even though the trees where they roosted were far away from where she was. The warm air was rich with the smells of summer, redolent with the scent of the moist earth, the marshy aroma of the mud flats, and the smell of someone grilling fish for lunch.

Lunch was a luxury unknown at Mitsuko's house, except to her father. Sometimes the littlest children were allowed to partake with him, but for everyone else, it was two meals a day.

Mitsuko dragged their washtub over from where it sat with the other families' and began pounding and scrubbing the clothes, tucking her kimono up into her obi so it wouldn't get wet. She actually liked washing clothes; the water was cold and made a nice, chuckling sound as it ran over the stones and around her legs. Sometimes there were other women there, too, and she could chat with them a little, maybe even sing a song or two, keeping rhythm as they scrubbed.

The river was deserted this late in the morning, though, so Mitsuko finished as quickly as she could, piled the wet clothes back on to her back and went home, calling Hanako over to help pull in the clean clothes and hang up the wet ones.

Her brother was fussing, so she put him on her back to get the clothes hung up.

"What did you do with it?" Hanako asked as they worked quickly at their task.

"With what?" Mitsuko asked, bouncing her brother a bit to keep him happy until her mother returned so she could nurse him from her old and saggy breasts.

"The letter!" Hanako said, as if it should be obvious.

"Oh!" Mitsuko thought. She honestly couldn't remember. "Did you give it back to me?"

"Yes, I did," Hanako told her. "Are you saying you lost it? An admirer's letter? Nēsan, you didn't!"

"I must've left it inside," Mitsuko said, shrugging, smiling over her shoulder at her baby brother.

"Be sure you put it away before Ma finds it," Hanako advised her.

Mitsuko nodded, reaching for the last diapers, tying them to the line. "You're right."

She shook her head to herself. *An admirer's letter.* What a notion.

6

A SELFISH DAUGHTER

The doors to their house were thrown open, a sign proclaiming their shame to all:

Auction Today. All usable furnishings and housewares

Fifteen-year-old Mitsuko looked around her. The wall she faced was dirty and peeling, bare except for the framed drawing of the Buddha that hung from a nail. A shiny white price tag dangled from it like a newly pulled tooth. Those same tags hung off nearly everything in the room. She bit her lip and went outside, but it was even worse than being in the house.

Two small boys stood in the dirt road, staring and laughing. She heard one say to the other, "Her pa spent everything they had on saké and geishas. Now they're going to have to go live in the Murakamis' barn, with their animals."

Mitsuko sighed. Her father, always in trouble in the village, had gotten into enormous debt, and the town council had finally gotten involved. His only skill, such as it was, as a mediocre weaver of grasses, was next to useless compared to the immense debt he'd accrued, and their meager possessions were being sold to begin the process of getting them out of it.

The boys were still staring. Mitsuko stared back at them until they ran away. Her mother shuffled out of the house behind her, and they stood together, silent. The autumn afternoon was filled with the acrid smell of burning leaves, and the sky spread out before them in a blaze of smoky orange, as if it were on fire.

Her mother put her hand on Mitsuko's arm. "You'd better come inside and help finish preparing for tomorrow."

They turned and went back into the house. There wasn't much left to do. Everything that could be sold had a tag on it already, and what little that was left wasn't worth selling, or owning, probably.

Mitsuko looked around at her brothers and sisters, most of whom were already sleeping. She pulled out her pallet and joined them, hoping she could get at least a little sleep, but morning came all too soon, the traitorous sun peeking over the horizon and into their crowded house before she'd even begun to feel rested.

Her family began to stir and rise, so she joined them, partaking of the sparse morning meal and getting the pallets put away before people started showing up to pick over their belongings, to gloat over her family's shame.

By late morning, most of the bigger items were gone, and only the most useless things were left; it was kind of sad to find that people didn't want to buy things that had been owned and treasured by her family for years and years, Mitsuko reflected.

In the afternoon, Mitsuko's little sister Fujiko ran into the house, gasping for breath. "Mr. Ōtake is coming. He's coming to buy the *tatami* maker, everyone says." She stood and looked around at the rest of her family. Mitsuko leaned against the wall. They were all there, except for her father, who had refused to be home for the auction. He had gone to the tavern in the next village.

Mr. Ōtake was one of the wealthiest men in the village, a merchant with two children who lived in a fine house and frequently lent Mitsuko's father money.

Mitsuko looked at her mother. She looked like a gray, shrunken ghost. Her dust-colored hair was gathered in a limp bun, from which web-like strands escaped. She tried ineffectually to tuck these strands back as she stood up and straightened her kimono.

There was a noise from the other room, and Fujiko, who was peeking through the doorway, turned back and said, "It's him, he's here!" in an excited whisper. Her mother hurried out to greet him. Mitsuko followed her, and stood just inside the next room, watching.

"Good day, Ōtake-san." Her mother, bowed, a deep, formal bow that brought her forehead parallel to the floor.

He acknowledged her with an offhand inclination of his head while he continued his examination of the tatami maker. He wore a new kimono, which had been made especially for the autumn in hues of brown, with accents of yellow and orange. His top coat looked elegant and machine made. The rich scent of his pipe filled the air. Mitsuko tried not to stare at him.

He turned to Mitsuko's mother. "Have you had an offer for this yet?" He rested a proprietary hand on the machine.

"No. The truth is that we really don't want to sell it." Mitsuko's mother said. She couldn't help but sound a little apprehensive.

"Oh?" Ōtake-san looked thoughtful. "And yet it has a price tag on it. Aren't you required to sell it?"

"Well," Mitsuko's mother began, "we would have to sell it

if someone made an offer." Her hands nervously twisted the sleeve of her kimono.

"Well then," Ōtake-san said.

"But it is our livelihood, Ōtake-san," said Mitsuko's mother. "If you force us to sell it, our children will surely starve." She looked at him beseechingly. Mitsuko wanted to die of shame.

Ōtake-san made a noise. He looked at Mitsuko, who hadn't moved from her place. "It doesn't look like she's starving to me."

"She's my oldest girl. She's always been healthy. But look at my other children." Mitsuko's mother gestured toward the doorway, where Mitsuko's brothers and sisters stood. Fujiko stood in front, dirty legs poking out from under her too-short kimono. "Look at her, my youngest girl." She gestured, and Fujiko came forward. "Open your mouth," she commanded.

Fujiko opened her mouth.

"Look at those teeth. Rotten! From not eating enough vegetables," her mother declared. "And her joints! This child will surely get rickets before she's ten."

Ōtake-san looked Fujiko over while she stood there with her mouth open like a fish. Then he looked back at Mitsuko.

"You! Aren't you the girl who cleans house for Dr. Sato?" he asked.

Mitsuko nodded and looked at the floor.

"Hmm." Ōtake-san stroked his chin. "He said you were the best maid he'd ever had." He took two steps to stand in front of Mitsuko. "Open your mouth."

Mitsuko looked at her mother, who only nodded impatiently. Mitsuko opened her mouth. Ōtake-san peered inside it for a moment, then he leaned back, apparently satisfied with the state of her teeth, and turned back to her mother.

His face looked young and smooth as silk, though he had to be close to her parents in age. His lips were closed around the pipe in a little knot as he sucked on it, then he smiled, showing that his own teeth were even and straight as matched pearls.

"I'm willing to forego making a bid on the tatami maker, if you will let me hire your daughter here to work for me. She will come live with us. As you have pointed out, she is very healthy, and she has all of her teeth. No one else in the village will be able to afford to bid on the tatami maker. What do you think of such an arrangement?"

Mitsuko saw the top of her mother's dusty gray head as she once again bowed deeply. "My husband and I would be most grateful for such an arrangement, Ōtake-san."

Ōtake-san made a sound of satisfaction. "Wonderful. My wife has been complaining about not having good household help. Hopefully this will put the matter to rest."

Mitsuko listened, keeping her face expressionless, as was her custom. She felt Hanako's hand searching for hers among the folds of her kimono sleeve and grasped it, grateful for the warmth.

As soon as Ōtake-san left, Mitsuko's mother sent one of her brothers to the council to tell them of this new turn of events, asking if the auction could be canceled. Word came back almost immediately that if they were going to keep their tatami maker, indeed the auction could be canceled, and the rest of their possessions would be saved.

By evening, it was all official, and new promissory notes had been put in place, with the tatami maker as collateral. Mitsuko's future wages were put into the pot, and shame for the family was avoided. Mitsuko's mother explained all of this to her father when he returned to the house that night.

He listened as he sat at the table, eating his dinner. One

of her little brothers sat next to him, having some miso soup. Her father nodded solemnly. "Good, this is a good thing," he intoned. "It's a good thing that she can do something to redeem herself, after the shame she's brought to us.

"Mitsuko! Come!" His voice shook the thin walls. "You're being given a chance to show that you can be a good girl, obedient, instead of the headstrong and selfish person you have hiding inside of you."

She stood and listened in silence, staring at the floor.

"You must try harder to be honest and open, to think of your family and not always of yourself," he instructed, setting his chopsticks across his rice bowl, indicating he was finished.

"Yes," she responded, quickly clearing his bowls from in front of him. As she left, she unthinkingly placed her brother's empty miso bowl on top of the stack.

She suddenly found herself on the floor, looking at the familiar leg of the table again as she raised her hand to her stinging cheek. She lay, unmoving, listening to her father's voice.

"What are you doing? You must never stack anyone's bowls on top of mine! I am the master of this house, and that will never change."

She waited until she was sure he was gone. Then she rose, shook her head to clear it, and picked up the crockery that was scattered about the room. Her sister, who had seen and heard the whole exchange, was already scrubbing the spilled food up off the floor.

Mitsuko left the following day, without a backward look to the house she'd left so many times. After leaving her on the floor the night before, her father had gone to the Ōtake household to offer his humble thanks as well.

Mitsuko walked to the village and to the Ōtakes' house, standing just outside the gate as she looked up at it. It boasted blue roof tiles and white plaster. A large bay window looked out over the front garden, and she could see an arrangement of chrysanthemums on a table inside. She stepped up to the door and rang the bell. Instead of the usual buzzing sound, she heard something that sounded like music, only played on bells. The door clattered open on its rollers, and a servant stared out at her.

"Aren't you the new maid?" she asked. At Mitsuko's nod, she said, "Servants must use the kitchen entrance unless they're accompanied by a member of the household." And the door was shut in her face.

Mitsuko went around to the kitchen and tapped on the door. She was let in to what was obviously the cooking area. It was warm and steamy, and Mitsuko could feel her pores begin to open. A real wood-burning stove stood in the middle of the room, and her nostrils were assaulted by the smell of the pork cooking under the broiler. She had only had pork once before, and she could still remember how rich it had tasted, how extravagant. Her mouth began to water.

She was mercifully led out of the kitchen and down a long passageway. Watery afternoon sunlight poured through numerous windows and shone on the polished hardwood floor, which gave off a smell of pine.

She was led to the front room, the one that held the chrysanthemums, and told to enter. An older woman and a young girl turned around at her approach. The older woman gestured her closer, then spoke.

"Mitsuko? I am Mrs. Ōtake, and this is the daughter of

the house, Hideko. " She indicated the girl sitting next to her, who inclined her head slightly in acknowledgement. Mrs. Ōtake continued to speak in a voice so devoid of country accent that for a moment Mitsuko couldn't understand her. "I believe you are the same age. Your main responsibility will be to attend her, although you will have other household duties, of course." She smiled for the first time. "Dr. Sato recommended you most highly to us. I hope you will be happy here."

Mitsuko looked at Hideko. She was slender as a reed, with long, graceful limbs. The skin that covered her arms, and even the skin on her face, had the look of porcelain. She was white in a way that could only come from indoor living, and her hands looked soft and unused.

"Thank you, Ōtake-san, Miss Hideko."

7

THE SECRET STUDENT

In the darkness, Mitsuko crept from her bed and noiselessly slid her bedroom door open. She padded down the hallway, stopping every now and then to listen. She had lived in this house for four months, and she knew that no one would be up this late.

She opened the door to Nobuhiro's room. Nobuhiro was Hideko's nine-year-old brother. She stood still for a moment, listened for his deep breathing, then tiptoed over to his desk. Next to it stood a trash basket. She carefully put her hand in it and felt all along the bottom. Her fingers closed around a small stick-shaped object, about five or six centimeters in length, and pointed on one end. She cautiously extracted her hand, looked at Nobu's sleeping form, and returned noiselessly to her room.

There, she took several items out of a drawer and laid them out on her futon: a notebook made out of old newspapers she had sewn together, an eraser that had been worn to an oblong the size of a throat lozenge, a candle stub, a packet of matches, and a battered high school textbook. To them she added her most recent acquisition, the pencil stub she had retrieved from Nobu's wastebasket. She struck a match and lit the candle. The flame flared briefly like a flower, illuminating her treasures. She propped the textbook open against her pillow, opened her newspaper notebook, and began to write.

This was a risky, dangerous game she played. She had been forbidden from studying, from learning any more. Her duties had been plainly laid out; she was to see to Miss Hideko's daily needs and keep house, doing whatever chores were asked of her. Schooling had no part in her day.

Her heart cried out for more, however. She thought of the omawarisan who had come calling last summer, who had given her the lovely letter with the poem. He would certainly never be interested in a lowly maid. Even though her circumstances had changed, and she was hopefully no longer destined for life on a subsistence-level farm, she was only marginally better off.

She strained her eyes, trying to make out the print of the old textbook in the dim light cast by the candle. The candle had been pilfered from the kitchen, a tiny end destined for the trash heap; it couldn't be missed, could it? The matches, too, had been stolen from the drawer in the kitchen, but, again, Mitsuko was hoping no one would notice. The pencil and eraser were taken from actual garbage cans, so surely no one would notice they were gone, and her "notebook" was of her own making, constructed of old newspapers sewn together so she could write between the lines. Who would complain about that?

But still she worried, jumping at every sound in the darkness. She read slowly through the lesson, her lips moving as she whispered the words to herself. She was lucky that she had her own "room." It was a storage area next to the kitchen where the bags of rice were kept, barely insulated and bitterly cold. The dust from the rice made her sneeze, but she had it to herself, and for this she was grateful. Her only concern was that she'd accidentally set fire to something with the candle.

Sometime in the middle of the night, she completed the lesson. She turned the page, longing to continue her studying, but she knew she had to sleep a little to have some energy for her chores the next day. Reluctantly, she closed the book, hid her precious items, and blew out the candle. She buried herself in her skimpy futon and closed her eyes.

She thought about what she'd studied that night. The lesson had been about botany, about flowers and how they were propagated. Apparently, a person could brush the pollen from one flower onto another and then wrap the flower up, waiting until a seed pod formed before gathering the seeds to plant in another location.

Who would even have thought such a thing was possible? And why? Why wouldn't you just let them pollinate themselves and wait to see what kind of flowers bloomed?

Mitsuko was mystified by this process.

She tried to imagine a world in which such things were important enough for people to get paid to study them in laboratories, in which people cared about the colors and numbers of petals on flowers, more than, say, how to grow bigger potatoes or more grains of rice.

She was awakened the next day by the sound of rain drumming on the roof of the house and sighed, knowing that she wouldn't be working outside. She got out of bed and quickly got dressed, braiding her long hair and winding it in a bun, pinning it up out of her way. She spent the day cleaning the house and attending Hideko, finally dressing her for her flower arranging class.

Imagine, a class just to learn how to place flowers in a

vase or shallow bowl of water so they looked their best, just so people could *look* at them. Mitsuko tried, and failed, to envision a life where money was spent so a person could learn to display flowers to their best advantage, placing them to face this way or that, so someone else could decide if they'd done a good job showing them off.

Mitsuko loved flowers, their beauty, their delicacy, how they would only bloom if the roots were healthy, the branches and leaves were cared for, if they had enough water and sun. If and only if everything else was *just right* would a person be rewarded with a splash of color, for just a few days, something special to enjoy for a moment before it would disappear, like it had never existed, a fleeting prize, sometimes even with a fragrance added as a bonus. And Hideko got to go and touch them, be surrounded by them, immersed in them, because of the accident of her birth, while Mitsuko scrubbed floors and waited for her return.

Around that time, Mitsuko went outside to wait for her. A cold winter rain pounded down, the drops bouncing off the pavement to wet the hem of Mitsuko's kimono. Her right hand was tucked up inside her sleeve, but her left hand, which clenched the handle of an umbrella, was numb from the cold, the knuckles showing white against the black wooden grip.

As she stood there, she saw her mother step out into the street from the kitchen entrance. She had come today, as she came every payday, to collect Mitsuko's wages, what little was left over after payment was made against what her father still owed. Their eyes met, and her mother nodded to her, then she turned and started walking home, hunched against the rain.

Mitsuko stepped back against the front gate to let a carriage pass, then stepped out again, peering through the rainy, wet afternoon for the Ōtake family carriage. It rounded the corner and pulled up at the gate. The door opened, and Mitsuko held the umbrella out over the opening. Hideko stepped out, resplendent in a vivid yellow kimono, a golden splash of springtime in the midst of the drab, gray winter.

"Welcome home, Hideko-san," Mitsuko murmured with a bow. "Your flower arranging class went well, I hope."

Hideko nodded and smiled her thanks. She passed through the gate and hurried to the door, then waited until Mitsuko opened it for her.

Mitsuko followed her inside, then hurried to get her shoes off and boil the water for Hideko's tea. She was just putting the kettle on when she heard her name called.

"Miiitsuuukoooo, where are you?"

Mitsuko hurried into Hideko's room. Hideko was standing in the middle of it, arms held out from her sides. Mitsuko rushed forward and with deft fingers untied the obi that held Hideko's kimono closed.

"Thank you, Mitsuko," she said. "I must get these clothes dried before the rainwater stains them."

Mitsuko only nodded as she unwrapped the kimono and finished undressing her mistress. Later, as she was spreading the clothes to dry, she found some fragrant camellias in the kimono sleeve, their stems cut for flower arranging. Mitsuko cupped the flowers in her hands, then lifted them to her nose, inhaling the sweet fragrance. She put them in her pillow, and went to sleep with their scent in her heart.

The next day, she once again stood outside, without the umbrella this time, and bowed deeply as she saw her mistress off to her daily calligraphy lessons. The cold, winter wind blew her hair around her face, pulling the black strands out of their bun and whipping them on her weathered cheek.

She had seen Hideko's script. It was bland and characterless, like worms crawling across the page. It was, however, correct, unlike her own. Mitsuko had no one to teach her the right way, unlike her mistress, who had the advantage of fresh brushes and ink every week, and instructors to show her how.

Someday, Mitsuko swore to herself. Someday she would have a brush, and the blackest, freshest of ink stones, and an instructor to show her how to hold the brush, and sheets and sheets of blank paper on which to practice, and she would be a master of calligraphy, renowned for her brushwork.

"Oh, it's cold today," Hideko declared as she settled into the carriage. "Get inside, Mitsuko, before you freeze!" Her tinkling laugh was carried away with the leaves.

Mitsuko nodded, bowing again.

As soon as the carriage was gone, Mitsuko got the broom and began to sweep the drive and the street in front of the house. It was pointless on a day like today. There was simply too much wind, and fresh debris was deposited as fast as she cleaned it up. This was the task she'd been given, however, and she performed it arduously.

"Ishikawa-san! I was hoping I would see you!"

Mitsuko heard the exuberant voice and knew who it was immediately. She didn't want to turn around, but she knew that she had to. She took a deep breath, stopped sweeping, and turned, trying and failing to tuck her hair back into its bun.

It was Murata-san, the nice young policeman. He looked very handsome in his uniform, rosy-cheeked from the cold and freshly-scrubbed, as usual.

"Good day," she said, looking down with a slight smile.

"Good day," he replied, moving from one foot to the other. "I heard from your sister that you were lately working here. I hope it's a nice change of pace, and that the work agrees with you? You're enjoying it?"

Mitsuko knew that everyone in the whole village was aware of why she was here, how she'd ended up as a maid to the wealthiest family in town. It was nice of him to feign ignorance, though.

"Yes, thank you," she replied. "It's nice to be working indoors most of the time, instead of on a farm, like before." That was true, at least.

"Ishikawa-san? Maybe you'll be able to continue your education in a few years," Murata-san said gently, his voice barely audible over the howling wind. He reached out and touched her sleeve.

Mitsuko kept her eyes on the street between them. How did he know about that?

She finally nodded, continuing to stare at the gravel pavement.

"Well, it was very nice to see you," Murata-san said cheerfully. "Until next time, then," he said, bowing a farewell.

Mitsuko bowed as well, taking care to do so a bit lower and a bit longer, as he was both a man and a person in a uniform.

She finally put the useless broom away and went to her room, where she saw the camellia petals still strewn about her pillow. She felt the tears, hot and bitter, roll down her cheeks and drip off her chin. In a fit of frustration, she slapped at the petals, scattering them all over. After a few minutes, though, she gathered them carefully, smoothing out the creases where she'd crushed them, arranging them once more around her pillow so she could smell them as she fell asleep.

That night, Mitsuko was awakened by scuffling at her door. She heard it open, then felt someone lie down next to her in the cold darkness, felt someone putting their hands on her.

She automatically put her hands up and clapped her legs together, holding them closed as tightly as she could.

"Eh, what are you doing?" a deep voice grumbled. "You're old enough for a bit of fun, aren't you? A plain girl like you should be glad someone takes a little interest, come on now."

"No, I don't want to," Mitsuko whispered, pushing the hands away. "It's a dangerous time of the month for me, I could lose my position, and it's a good job, my entire family is counting on me."

She had seen some of the men who worked on the property looking at her, but she had hoped that being a stout girl with a country accent would keep her safe.

Obviously not.

She rolled away, holding her sleeping kimono closed, repeating that she didn't want to, that it was a dangerous time.

Somewhere in the house a door closed loudly, making the man with her jump up.

"You'd better go before you get caught," Mitsuko whispered loudly. "We'll both get fired."

The man left without another word, and the next morning Mitsuko asked for a lock to be put on her door as extra safety against thieves who might want to come in the night and take the precious rice from where it was stored.

A bolt that could be shot from the inside was put in before the end of the day.

8

THE BEST MAID

Mitsuko (in the middle) with two of her sisters and a niece, ca 1933

"Ōtake-san?" Mitsuko entered the room where Mr. Ōtake sat reading the paper. As usual, the smell of his pipe surrounded him. The windows were open, and every so often, the warm spring breeze carried cherry blossom petals into the room.

Mitsuko had lived in this house for two years. She had let herself go dead inside, choking her dreams, smothering them with dust, drowning them with her tears. It was less painful than trying to nurture them, pitiful things that they were. She didn't think about her little house with the flowers on the table, where she could live alone, or even with a special someone, who used to look like the nice policeman whose face she no longer exactly remembered.

Her days were a never-ending stream of chores, of dressing and undressing her mistress, a young girl her own age, of cleaning the same floors, of dusting the same furniture, of slopping out the same toilets, and always, always, the smell of food she couldn't have, the sight of books she could never read, let alone own, the sound of beautiful music she could never play; the list went on and on and on.

But she'd seen an advertisement last week that had stopped her in her tracks, that had gotten her thinking.

Mr. Ōtake put his newspaper down and looked at her. "Yes, Mitsuko?"

"I am very grateful to you for letting me work here. I know that we still owe you a lot of money." She took a deep breath.

He nodded.

"Well, I have heard that there's a school in Kichijoji, in Tokyo, that trains women to be nurses and midwives. If you could advance the money for me to go there, then I could repay you much more quickly."

She stared at him, watching for his reply.

"Of course," she continued, "if you're against this, I will willingly work for you until the debt is repaid." She knew that such a thing would never have occurred to him on his own. She also knew that a plan like this might appeal to him. She'd heard him commenting to his wife that he thought Mitsuko to be "quick of wit," and probably capable of more than being a mere maid.

"Let me think about it for a few days." He got back to his newspaper, and Mitsuko turned and left the room. Hope bloomed inside her as it hadn't for years. She hadn't discussed it with her mother, nor had it occurred to her to do such a thing. Her mother would have scoffed, anyway. Why take such a risk? Better to pay off a debt honestly, scrubbing floors with your own two hands, she would've said.

This was the way her mother always lived her life, frightened, never looking past the next meal, the next payday, no imagination. And Mitsuko knew her father would say the same thing. Why? Why change what was working? She was chipping away at the debt, week by week, month by month, it would be paid off in twenty or thirty years, wouldn't it? What was the problem?

They didn't care that some days Mitsuko lost sensation in her fingertips from the lye that she used to scrub, or that her back never stopped aching from one day to the next from being bent over to carry the heavy loads. Life was made to be endured, for working hard, they would have said. She needed to stop complaining and do what she was supposed to do for once in her life, they would have said.

Mitsuko knew that one of her younger brothers had started going to school in the village. Not that she begrudged him this privilege. As far as she was concerned, all of her siblings should be going to school, every single day, learning to read and write and do sums and multiplication tables, learning about the big world around them. But she felt like her own chance at learning, at knowledge, was slipping away, like a window was closing for her somehow. Who ever heard of a seventeen-year-old going to school? Or worse, a twenty-year-old?

How could she possibly learn everything she needed to know? All of the knowledge that existed out there in the world, all of the facts? The thousands of flowers and plants that were out there growing, *right now*, would forever remain nameless for her, her chance at learning about them gone, poof, like a puff of smoke. There were libraries filled with books just *bursting* with facts that would remain out of her reach *forever*, if she didn't start soon. These thoughts drove Mitsuko mad with frustration.

The children of the house where she worked hated school, hated all of the lessons they had to take. They did everything they could to get out of going, particularly the boy, including feigning sickness. Mitsuko thought he must be out of his mind. She would have given anything, *anything*, to spend her days just living and going to school and learning.

The plan to go to Kichijoji to learn nursing and midwifery in order to pay off her family's debt more quickly was Mitsuko's last-ditch attempt to obtain her freedom so she could just start, somehow, to learn what the world had to teach her. Please, please, she begged in her heart of hearts, let Mr. Ōtake agree to her plan. She waited, day after day, for the master of the house to call her into his study and tell her his decision. After one week, she was worried that he'd forgotten all about it; after ten days, she was all but sure.

Finally, on a warm spring evening, she heard the words she'd been waiting to hear:

"Mitsuko? Come in my study, please. I have something to say to you."

Two weeks later she left for Kichijoji, saying nothing to her parents of her change of plans.

9

SETTLING IN

Mitsuko at the midwifery school in Kichijoji, 1934

Mitsuko arrived at the dormitory in the spring of 1934, ready to learn, ready to begin this next chapter in her life. She had to answer to no one but herself, had no brothers or sisters to look after, no clothes to wash or iron that weren't her own, and kept her own schedule.

The other girls at the midwifery school in Kichijoji often complained about sleeping six to a room. Mitsuko kept her mouth shut but frequently wondered what kind of opulent circumstances they'd come from that this luxurious room with three sets of actual bunk *beds,* and not mere pallets on the floor, would be considered a hardship.

She luxuriated in the communal bath, where they all bathed, with the taps that poured *hot water* at the turn of a spigot, at the actual tiled tubs that were full of said hot water *every night,* and not just once a week. She loved having her own cake of soap, her own rough towel with which to dry herself, and her very own bed, with sheets that she could wash in the morning and hang, that would be waiting for her, clean and dry, every night.

Life was good.

And that didn't even take into account the fact that she was allowed to study, to learn, every blessed day. Her teachers, those amazing people, poured knowledge into her soul like a good drink from a large pitcher, every day, and she accepted it gratefully. She learned the mysteries of the female body, of their menstrual cycles, their anatomy, the myths and facts surrounding the fearful events of childbirth.

Being a teenaged girl in rural 1930s Japan had given Mitsuko a skewed perspective on life in general, she realized. Coming to Tokyo to study at seventeen had been one of the luckiest things that could've happened to her. She wondered some nights, as she lay on her bottom bunk, listening to her five roommates snore around her, what would've become of her if Mr. Ōtake hadn't agreed to her plan.

How had she gotten so lucky?

Her dorm mother, Yamada-san, was really only a "mother" in title; she was in fact rather brash and scary. Yamada-san was a woman in her forties who liked to drink and gossip, and who didn't seem to feel particularly motherly towards the twenty-four young women in her care.

The nurses-in-training were for the most part very serious and focused on their studies, so Yamada-san didn't have much to do, which seemed to be exactly how she liked it.

The first night Mitsuko spent in the dorm, she was in bed mending some of her old clothes before going to sleep. She had her very own lamp that clipped to her iron bed frame that she was allowed to leave on until eleven PM, which was the official lights-out time.

It was heaven to Mitsuko.

Yamada-san went from bed to bed, making sure the girls were properly attired and where they belonged.

"Ito-san, please make sure that your reading material is always appropriate for a future nurse and midwife? Thank you." She moved on to the next bed.

"Eguchi-san, writing to your family? Wonderful."

She stopped at Mitsuko's bed. "Ishikawa-san, you sew beautifully; your stitches are so even and small."

"Thank you, Yamada-san," Mitsuko responded, wondering what the older woman wanted. In Mitsuko's experience, compliments usually came at a price.

Sure enough, the next night, Yamada-san approached Mitsuko with a small bag of mending. "I was hoping you wouldn't mind to do a bit of mending for me? Since it seems to come so easily to you? Thank you so much."

Within a few weeks, Mitsuko knew she was doing mending and sewing that wasn't Yamada-san's own, as some of the things weren't even women's clothing. Every night, after a day spent in classes, she returned to find Yamada-san's bag of clothes at the foot of her bed and opened it to begin that night's needlework. Every morning she would leave the previous night's work neatly folded in the bag, with the bag hanging from her bedpost. That night, when she returned from dinner, the bag would be on her bed, filled with more sewing for her to do.

One day, she passed Yamada-san's office and heard her talking to Nakamoto-sensei, the headmistress of the school and one of the first women in the whole country to hold such a position. Mitsuko revered her and hoped to meet her and thank her in person someday for the opportunity to attend her school and pursue her studies.

"Oh no, Sensei," Yamada-san was saying. "It's honestly my pleasure to do something to make your busy life even a little bit easier, truly."

"Well, I wanted to stop by and thank you in person," Nakamoto-sensei said. "I'm kept running around from morning until night, as you know, and I certainly don't have time to do such things as mending, and you have a very delicate touch with the needle, I never knew! Your stitches are exquisite, I must say, Yamada-san."

Yamada-san's laugh was high-pitched and grated on Mitsuko's ears. "No, no, of course not! Now my mother's handiwork was truly beautiful, Sensei, I wish you could've seen it. Mine looks so clumsy and awkward by comparison. Like I said, however, I'm very happy to do whatever I can to help you in any way."

"Well, thank you again, I'm very grateful."

Mitsuko quickly stepped back against the wall to let Sensei pass, bowing her head as she stepped out of Yamada-san's office. She waited until Sensei had gone by to continue on her way.

Even having Yamada-san take credit for her needlework was something Mitsuko could live with; she considered it part of the price of her new life in Kichijoji, just a small thing she had to endure in order to enjoy her clean, comfortable bed, her hot baths, the chance to study every day, and the joy of walking around the shops on the random Sunday afternoon.

The only dark cloud in her life came when her parents found out what she'd done, found out about the new life she'd finagled for herself without consulting them, and wrote to her about it.

Dear Mitsuko,

I suppose you think you're clever to have arranged this easy and fun new situation, once again with no thought for anyone but yourself. You realize that, while you're off in Tokyo 'studying,' you're bringing in no money at all, and getting us even deeper in debt? That for the next two years all you are is another problem for us to solve? And we hear that you're actually trying to take extra certificates in things that aren't even related to nursing while you're there!

You have always been the most headstrong, willful and stubborn child, the most self-centered and selfish of all the children, always thinking of only yourself. We don't understand why this is so.

It should be an honor for you to be the one to help the family, to work to help us, yet you insist, every time you get the chance, to put yourself first. We will never understand this.

Someday you will marry and be a bride, and you will no longer be our problem to solve, your shame will no longer be ours to bear. Perhaps then you'll understand what we're talking about. Until then, you are a member of this household, and your behavior is a reflection on us. Please try to remember this always.

If you receive any payment for work, please send it along, as it is greatly needed at home.

Your parents in respect.

·   ·   ·

MITSUKO PUT the letter away and didn't respond to it, as there was really nothing she could say, but when she received her next two weeks' wages for doing clerical work at the clinic where she worked part-time, she sent the money to her mother with no note. She continued to do this, every other pay period, until she got her nurse-midwife-in-training job one year later.

Mitsuko (far left) with some of her fellow students at the midwifery school in Kichijoji, 1933

10

MIDWIFE-IN-TRAINING

Mitsuko when she was working as a nurse and midwife, ca 1943

"Today you begin your practical training as midwives," their instructor told them, her voice strong and serious. "All of you are ready to do this medically, but not all of you are ready emotionally. We're going to find out who you really are. Many of you won't make it past today, but rather will be sent home in disgrace. Are you ready for this?"

"Yes, Sensei," the class responded, bowing deeply.

Mitsuko bowed along with her classmates, but inside she told herself she would not, absolutely would not, get sent home. Quitting or being asked to leave was not an option for her. She was not like the other girls in the program, who had regular college or sweethearts waiting for them. She would only have years of drudgery and misery awaiting her, a lifetime of work on her hands and knees as a maid, cooking and cleaning, sweeping up after someone else. This beautiful vista of independence and knowledge would be gone.

This day, this practical training, put her one day closer to her neat little house for one with the table and the window with the vase, the vase where she would keep flowers all year round. Now the dream had changed a little bit, for the flowers in the vase had been artfully arranged by Mitsuko herself, and there was a scroll on the wall with calligraphy that Mitsuko had written, the brushstrokes recognized by everyone as superior workmanship, with a special drawer underneath where she would keep her own special brush and inkstone, and only the best quality paper.

Mitsuko gathered her midwifery kit and followed the woman who would be her supervisor for the duration of the training. Her name was Hoshikawa-san, a stout woman in her late thirties with a salt-and-pepper bun and a kind, no-nonsense manner.

"Hello, nice to meet you," Mitsuko said, bowing lower and longer to Hoshikawa-san, her acknowledged superior. "I hope to learn much from you in the future. Thank you for taking the time to teach such an undeserving pupil as myself," she said in conclusion, using the standard words for greeting a teacher for the first time, and the politest honorific language she could.

"Hello, and please don't bother with honorifics when talking to me, Ishikawa-san," Hoshikawa-san responded with a broad smile as she threw her leg over her bike. Mitsuko noticed that she had a gap between her two front teeth, which made her smile seem even more friendly. "We're going to get very familiar with each other very quickly doing the work we do, so using simple politeness when you talk will be fine. There's your bicycle over there." She pointed. "You know how to ride a bike, right?"

Mitsuko nodded.

"Good. Let's go, we have a busy morning."

Mitsuko was exhausted by the time the morning was half over. She lost track of the number of houses they visited. Some of the households were poor, some were middle-class, some were well-kept, some were dirty; the only thing they had in common was that a woman who was close to giving birth lived in them.

"Ishikawa-san, make some tea, please," Hoshikawa-san requested at the second house. Mitsuko was surprised, because the mother-to-be had made it at the first house. Then she looked around, and saw how filthy the place was, and realized that Hoshikawa-san probably didn't want the person who lived there touching what they would be drinking.

Mitsuko quickly and efficiently rinsed out the pot and some cups. She found the canister of tea leaves and shook some into the pot while she put the kettle on the stove to boil. While she was doing all this, she watched Hoshikawa-san examine the mother-to-be, paying attention to the language the older woman used to get the patient to relax, in what order the various questions were asked, and how she kept her hands clean to perform the various tasks.

Mitsuko herself helped where she could, making Hoshikawa-san's job easier, staying out of the way when she knew she'd be a hindrance. Some of the houses they visited were so dirty Mitsuko couldn't believe anyone would want to bring a new baby into them, but she held her tongue and did her job to the best of her ability. Some of the mothers-to-be were younger than she was; indeed, some seemed barely old enough to be pregnant. Some must've been older than her mother, nearly too old for childbearing.

"You look ready to drop," Hoshikawa-san remarked at the end of the first day when they finally turned their bicycles toward their dormitory.

Mitsuko shook her head to indicate that this was not so, but her chin trembled, giving away her exhaustion and fatigue. She had seen so much for one day, so many different people from so many different stages of life.

"Don't worry, you'll get used to it," Hoshikawa-san assured her with a smile and a reassuring pat on her shoulder. "It's a lot for one day, but you'll see, you'll adjust soon."

Mitsuko just nodded as she settled herself on her bike, adjusting her midwifery kit on the back so it wouldn't fall off.

They pedaled away into the city dusk, joining the throngs of people heading home after a tiring day of work.

HER DAYS FELL into a routine fairly quickly, of rising while it was still dark so she could take her time getting ready for the day; she had spent enough of her life fighting for space and time at a sink with other people. She would much rather give up a little sleep and have some time to herself to wash up in peace and quiet, to have a little reflective time to sip her morning tea alone.

Then it was off to have breakfast in the bustling cafeteria with the rest of the students before heading out on her rounds with Hoshikawa-san. Sometimes her days were so busy that she didn't even have time to eat her lunch, which was fine with her. Hoshikawa-san was a veritable fount of experience and knowledge, and Mitsuko could listen and learn from her all day long. She knew she was lucky to have the gap-toothed woman as her supervisor. She'd heard horror stories from the other girls about some of their superiors. They showed up to their shifts drunk, they weren't competent instructors or midwives, they shifted too much responsibility too soon to their students, or they were simply mean women, shrill and domineering, who made the young trainees miserable from morning until night, sometimes reducing them to tears.

"ISHIKAWA-SAN, come, quickly, grab the baby's head," she was directed.

Mitsuko went around to the other side of the bed and did as she was told. The room was filled with the sharp, coppery smell of blood, but she'd long since ceased to notice such things. Steam rose from the basin, which she'd just filled with clean hot water.

"Once you have a good grip, tell mother to bear down and push as you turn, understand?"

"I understand," she responded briefly as she nodded. She put her hands around the slippery head and then told the mother to push as hard as she could during her next contraction. When she felt the mother pushing, she turned the baby, extending her grasp onto the shoulders as they were pushed out.

Within seconds, the baby boy was safely delivered, and she was cleaning and weighing him as Hoshikawa-san cleaned the mother.

Then she handed the baby into her waiting arms so she

and the other midwife could clean the bedding one last time and call the family into the room.

This was what everyone hoped for, the happy outcome, the time for giving thanks and burning incense and paying the visit to the temple to see the monk.

Mitsuko beamed at everyone as she and Hoshikawa-san packed up their kits to go on to the next house to do it all over again.

"Well, Ishikawa-san, you have done very well." The head of the midwifery school smiled at Mitsuko, who looked down at the ground, embarrassed.

"No, no, Sensei, you have been a better teacher than I deserved," Mitsuko protested, but her face was flushed with pleasure.

"Nonsense. You are one of the best pupils I've ever had. I don't think I've ever had a student who took the Midwifery Certificate and the Nursing Certificate simultaneously. And didn't you take a Flower Arranging Certificate at the same time as well?"

Mitsuko nodded, unable to control her smile.

"Well, I know you'll want to take a little time off, but as soon as you're ready, I can give you references to any hospital in Tokyo. Or Kawasaki, if you prefer." She smiled again at Mitsuko.

"Oh, thank you, Sensei, but I won't be taking any time off," said Mitsuko. She leaned forward in her chair, speaking eagerly. "I would like to take this week to go and see my family, my sister, and to thank the people who paid for my school, but after that I'll be ready to begin working."

The director looked at her in surprise. "Whatever you want, then. Just let me know."

"I will."

～

MITSUKO, accompanied by both her mother and father, walked from their house toward the Ōtakes'. Four years had passed since she'd first arrived there to work. She'd been a sixteen-year-old girl then; now she was a twenty-year-old woman. The house looked little changed. It was still the most elegant in the village.

They rang the bell and were admitted into the front room, the room where Mitsuko had first met Mrs. Ōtake and Hideko. Mr. and Mrs. Ōtake were waiting there for them.

Mitsuko, her mother, and her father all knelt on the floor in front of the Ōtakes.

"We have come," began her father without preamble, "to thank you for your kindness to our family. We know that we did not deserve such kindness, and we are most grateful." Mitsuko, her mother, and her father all bowed forward until their foreheads touched the floor. They remained that way until Mr. Ōtake spoke.

"Please, sit up, please. I assure you, it was our pleasure to sponsor such a bright girl, such a good girl." Mitsuko lifted her head and saw that the Ōtakes were smiling. Mr. Ōtake continued talking. "And now that you've finished school, do you have any plans?"

"I think that I will work as a nurse at a hospital in Kawasaki," Mitsuko answered.

"Kawasaki!" Mrs. Ōtake exclaimed. "That's so far away! What about your family? Do you want to be so far away from them?"

Mitsuko just stared at her. How, *how* was it possible to have spent so much time living in the same house, sharing the same dwelling, and not know what was in her heart? Did this clueless woman honestly not know that Mitsuko's only wish in life was to live free and alone, to not be told what to do?

Before Mitsuko had a chance to respond, Mr. Ōtake spoke again. "She's right. You can't go to Kawasaki. Who knows what might happen to you there?" He turned to her parents. "My wife and daughter were telling me just the other day about what a help your daughter was around here. 'I could always tell when Mitsuko had polished the hallway, she did such an excellent job,' my wife was saying. Isn't that right?" He looked at Mrs. Ōtake, who nodded.

Did they not, could they not, see how much she'd changed? Couldn't they tell that she was no longer the shy, retiring young girl who'd come to their house to be their maid? Didn't they see that the woman who sat before them was now a self-confident nurse and midwife, ready to go out into the world and make her way in it?

"She was the best maid we've ever had," Mrs. Ōtake said to Mitsuko's parents with a smile. "We haven't been able to find *anyone* to replace her."

"What do you say, Mitsuko?" Mr. Ōtake looked at her, still smiling. "Why don't you forget about Kawasaki for a little while and stay here and work for us?"

Mitsuko could only stare.

"But—but what about all of the money I owe you?" She felt like her kimono was too tight, like she couldn't breathe.

Mr. Ōtake waved a hand in an expansive gesture. "Don't worry about the money, you'll pay us back someday." He looked at her parents. "What do you think?"

Without hesitation, Mitsuko's father once again lowered

his head to the floor. "Thank you, I truly thank you, for all of the kindness you have shown to our family. It would mean a great deal to us to have her nearby."

Mitsuko tried to swallow with a throat that seemed to have stopped working. The beautiful vista that had opened up before her was receding at the speed of light.

"So! It's settled, then," said Mr. Ōtake, with a clap of his hands. "Mr. Ishikawa, would you share a drink of sake with me to celebrate your daughter's graduation, and her return to us?"

Mitsuko's father reached for the glass with a bow of thanks, as Mitsuko stumbled to her feet, legs numb.

Mrs. Ōtake smiled at her. "Why don't you come with me?"

As Mitsuko followed her down the familiar hallway, Mrs. Ōtake's words floated back to her as if she were dreaming. She could hear her chattering on about how she'd meant what she'd said, that the house had never been cleaner, Hideko had never been so beautifully turned out as when Mitsuko had been with them.

Mitsuko looked out of the windows in the hallway, and noticed for the first time that autumn was nearly over, and that winter was almost upon them.

11

A CITY GIRL

Mitsuko as a nurse and midwife in Kawasaki, ca 1940

The house was full of strangers, delivery people, packages, and strange rustlings and stirrings at odd times. The back room, which was normally reserved for formal occasions and contained the alcoves devoted to the church and family ancestors, was now full of gifts and bolts of cloth.

Mitsuko was kept at a dead run from when she woke until well into the night, when she would drop, exhausted, onto her pallet. Preparations had reached fever pitch for the upcoming nuptials of Hideko Ōtake. The daughter of the house was getting married, to the son of a wealthy merchant in a neighboring town, and everything was being done in style.

The only upside to all of this, as far as Mitsuko was concerned, was that, after the wedding, she might possibly be allowed to leave and go work as a nurse at the hospital in Kawasaki. As soon as she'd heard about the engagement, she'd approached the master of the house.

"Ōtake-san? May I speak with you?"

"Of course." He was slightly drunk and feeling expansive, having just celebrated his daughter's betrothal with the father of her new fiancé.

"After Hideko-san is married, she will of course be leaving your house and establishing a residence of her own," Mitsuko began. "She will surely want a proper lady's maid, not just a country girl who scrubs floors. And you have so many servants that I don't think you'll need to keep me full-time once she's gone. Perhaps this would be a good time for me to begin my nursing career...?" She trailed off uncertainly. This was as close as she could come to asking to be sent away.

"I could also pay off my family's debt faster," she reminded him cleverly. This had been the original plan, after all. By sending her to school, not only had she not made a dent in the debt, it had increased significantly. Mitsuko knew her mother had been coming at regular intervals to collect her wages, as much as could be spared at any given time, so the original amount couldn't possibly have shrunk by any notable amount.

He nodded, his liquor-reddened face looking serious. "You're right. You'd be wasted here."

Mitsuko bit back the urge to ask what she'd been doing here these last years, and merely looked down at the tatami.

"Yes, I've decided," Ōtake-san declared, nodding again.

"You will go begin your new life as a nurse after Hideko has gone to be a bride."

She let her breath out slowly and carefully.

THE TROLLEY PULLED up to the station where Mitsuko stood waiting. She declined when a well-dressed businessman politely offered her his seat inside, and walked through the car and out the narrow door to the back platform.

It was spring of 1937, and the cold April wind hit her like a wave bursting upon a rock, and she turned her face toward it, lifting her head into the sights and sounds of Kawasaki. She could see the people inside the trolley staring at her as she stood on the platform. She turned her back towards them, to look, as she did every morning, out at the huge city that was now her home. The sky was still a pale, pre-dawn pink, but Kawasaki was already bustling with life. The wind carried to her the faint smell of fish broiling, the slightly stronger odor of smoke from thousands of wood-burning stoves, and, strongest of all, the smell of exhaust from hundreds of newly imported automobiles.

As the trolley passed Kawasaki Station, Mitsuko saw people pouring out of the exits like ants, scattering in a thousand different directions as they headed to work.

To work.

Mitsuko's broad, flat face glowed as she thought of the phrase, and of what it meant. She was going to work, to give nursing care at a hospital. She would be paid wages, she would clock in and out at a specific time, and, as soon as her family's debts were paid, no one would own her. She would be free.

Mitsuko, a young professional, ca 1941

SHE HEARD the atonal voice of the trolley conductor, announcing her stop, and she regretfully stepped back inside to pay her fare before getting off.

That afternoon, as she was walking past the nurse's station, she heard someone calling her name. She turned and saw an orderly hurrying toward her.

"Your mother is here to see you."

Mitsuko nodded her thanks and strode toward the nurses' lounge. She slipped her hand into the pocket of her white uniform to make sure that the bills were still there.

The halls of the hospital bombarded her senses, from the glaring, bright lights to the astringent smells of rubbing alcohol and iodine.

'I am a part of this,' she thought to herself. 'I belong here.' She took a deep breath and pushed open the door of the lounge.

Her mother turned at the sound of the door. She was wearing a man's work shirt with a *happi,* or short kimono jacket, farmer's pants, and long, thick socks with *zoris.* Her hands looked reddened and chapped, and her fingernails were packed with dirt.

Mitsuko reached into her pocket for the money and

thrust it at her mother. "Here is what I have so far for this month. I'll mail you the rest when I have it." She turned to go, but her mother stopped her.

"Aren't you even going to offer your mother a cup of tea?" she asked. "I've been on a train all day." She began to count the money as Mitsuko put the kettle on for tea.

"One thousand yen!" Her mother chuckled as she put the money in her sleeve. "At this rate you will have paid off the debt in less than ten years!" To Mitsuko, her mother's country voice sounded unnaturally loud and coarse. She wondered if she sounded that way to others.

"I'll mail you the rest," she repeated.

But her mother was shaking her head. "Someone could steal it out of the mail. No, I think it's best if I come and get it in person."

"Please don't come here anymore." Mitsuko kept her back to her mother as she carefully measured tea leaves into the pot. The rich, slightly bitter aroma of green tea filled the air.

"Why not?" Her mother looked surprised.

Mitsuko finally turned to face her. "Look at you! Your hair is a mess, you're not even wearing real shoes, and your accent makes you sound like a country bumpkin!"

Her mother strode across the room to stand in front of her, raised her hand, and slapped Mitsuko's face, hard. "And just what do you think you sound like, anyway?" Their faces were only centimeters apart, and Mitsuko could see her mother's very clearly. White hair sprang away from her temples, framing a face that was covered with an intricate web of wrinkles. Milky cataracts were forming in her eyes.

Mitsuko slowly raised her hand to her stinging face. She lowered her head in apology. "You're right, I'm sorry."

She poured the tea in little cups, making sure to offer

her mother the first, and they drank in silence for about five minutes. Her mother then rose to go, saying that she would be back next month.

Mitsuko said nothing, but the next week she mailed her mother a dark brown dress and a pair of shoes to match.

THE NURSES WERE ENTITLED to one day off out of every seven, but Mitsuko never took one. The more she worked, she reasoned, the sooner the debt would be paid off. Besides, she didn't know anyone in the city, and if she weren't at the hospital earning money, she'd only be out in the city spending it.

As a result, she had very little time off; when she did, however, she would walk around Kawasaki, taking in the sights. The tall buildings, the bright lights, the hodgepodge of smells astounded her, but perhaps the most amazing thing of all was the noise. The sheer volume, the cacophony of the city, was incredible to her. The buses and cars, of course, were like noisy beetles, putting along the filthy streets, blowing their horns. Throw in the trains and street-cars, and the music coming from the businesses, and a person almost couldn't differentiate the sounds at all.

On top of all this, though, was the noise made by the people of the city; the population of Kawasaki topped 150,000. Mitsuko loved being part of this number, one of the cosmopolitan city-dwellers of modern Japan. Every time she returned to the nurses' dorm, the rooming house where she lived, whether it was from work or from her perambulations around Kawasaki, she would feel like she'd been buffeted by the sounds of the city.

"Where do you go, Mitsuko-san, all by yourself?" one of

her roommates asked curiously. Mitsuko already had some-what of a reputation at the hospital as a quiet person who didn't socialize at all. She had been pursued by a couple of doctors, and they'd been told the same thing, kindly, but firmly:

"Thank you so much for your invitation, but I have too many family commitments to think about seeing anyone socially."

Her roommates thought she was crazy to turn down actual doctors, who liked her because she was so hard working and healthy.

"Just out," she replied vaguely, smiling a secret smile to herself. She was going to be free.

She was.

12

A LATE-NIGHT SAVIOR

Over the heads of the sleeping patients came the sound of a bell. Light and silvery, this sound was curiously at odds with the sickroom atmosphere of the contagious diseases ward where Mitsuko worked.

She looked up from the powdered medicine she was measuring and, seeing that it was her patient, rose and went to her on silent, rubber-soled feet.

"Yes? What do you need?" She wiped the young girl's forehead with a cool cloth, and nodded at the girl's mother, who had been sleeping in a chair next to her daughter's bed.

"Please. My throat hurts. Can you give me some medicine?" The girl looked at Mitsuko out of eyes that were glazed with fever. Her breath, which had the sour tang of prolonged illness, came out in harsh rasps, as though she had swallowed gravel.

"That's just because your fever's been so high. I don't have any medicine for that." Mitsuko looked at the girl's chart.

"Please, Nurse," the girl's mother said. "Can't you do something for her?"

Mitsuko felt in her pocket and pulled out a tin of throat lozenges. She opened the tin, shook one out into her hand, and offered it to the girl. "Here. I've had a sore throat, too, and these have helped me." She lowered her voice to a conspiratorial whisper. "But don't tell anyone I gave it to you, okay?"

The girl nodded and gratefully accepted the lozenge. Mitsuko smiled at her, nodded to her mother, and returned to her station to finish measuring the medicine.

Later, near the end of her shift, the girl's mother came and sat down next to Mitsuko.

"Thank you for taking care of my daughter. You're a good nurse, and I think it helps her that you're so young, and close to her own age. Not many of the nurses on the contagious diseases ward are," she said with a smile.

The truth was that the pay for working on the CD ward was double that of the regular wards. Even this, however, wasn't enough enticement to get the younger nurses to risk infection themselves. Even with the precautions they took, it wasn't unheard of, and most of the younger nurses wouldn't even consider it.

"I'm very young and inexperienced," Mitsuko responded with a self-deprecating smile.

"I don't think that's true at all," the woman replied, shaking her head. "You are conscientious and dedicated, and such a hard worker. My daughter has been sick so often, and you are the best nurse she's ever had." She leaned forward and stared intently at Mitsuko for a moment, then continued. "Please pardon my rudeness, but are you married?"

Faintly, from the main lobby, Mitsuko could hear the clock strike eleven, and from just down the hall she could hear the laughter of one of the younger nurses intermingled with the deep voice of a doctor. Funny that she would be asked that question by a woman, when she was so used to hearing it from the doctors on the staff. She told the woman exactly what she had told the doctors.

"I'm afraid that I'm much too busy to be married to someone. I have family responsibilities."

The woman sat back in her chair, apparently satisfied. "Good. I would like to tell you about my brother. He is twenty-five, and not yet married. We have been looking for a healthy, hard-working wife for him for many years, but we haven't been able to find anyone. I think that you are just the person for him. What do you think?"

Mitsuko stared at her, the medicines forgotten. She thought of her future house, the one she'd been dreaming of. It was a one-person house, intended for her to live in alone. She even thought of Murata-san, who still wrote to her and sent her flowers. She never considered him seriously, but she would rather be married to him than a stranger she'd never met, someone who couldn't even be bothered to find his own wife.

The sound of the woman snapping her purse open brought Mitsuko back from her thoughts with a start.

"Here is my family address. Please write to us. And may I have your family's address?" The woman looked at Mitsuko expectantly.

"No, I'm sorry, there's no mail service to their village yet." Mitsuko felt the lie glide effortlessly off her tongue, tasting like oily butter.

The young girl to whom she'd given the lozenge was discharged the next day, and Mitsuko thought no more about the matter.

"Ishikawa-san, someone was here looking for you." The nurses' aide spoke in passing as she held the forms for Mitsuko to sign.

"Oh?" Mitsuko scribbled her signature on the drug forms and looked at the aide. "Who was it?"

"Her name was Yoshida. She said you were her daughter's nurse two years ago."

Mitsuko only looked blankly at the girl. Two years ago?

"She said she spoke to you about her brother," the aide explained patiently.

"Oh, yes, now I remember. Thank you for telling me." Mitsuko bit her lip in annoyance. "Did she say she'd be coming back?"

"No, she didn't say." The aide smiled. "It's nice, isn't it, when your old patients remember you? She probably wants to give you a present."

Mitsuko only nodded as she walked away. As she turned the corner, she heard the laughter well before she reached the group of doctors. She smiled in anticipation of hearing the joke.

"Here she is, the most popular nurse in the whole hospital," one of the doctors said as he laughed. "You should have told us that you were promised to someone else," he chided her. "Then we wouldn't have wasted our time asking."

Mitsuko's smile vanished, and she could feel a blush begin to creep up her neck.

"Come on, Ishikawa-san, don't be shy. Everyone knows that you have a fiancé, that you're secretly betrothed."

Mitsuko turned on her heel and walked to her supervisor's office. She knocked and entered.

"Please forgive my intrusion, but I must speak to you right away about a transfer."

Her supervisor looked surprised. "But why? Haven't you been happy here these last years?"

"I have been very happy here," Mitsuko replied. She bit her lip hard so she wouldn't cry. How could she explain, what words could she use to explain to this very kind woman that she didn't want to be married, that she didn't want to be pursued, that she just wanted to be *left alone*? If the Yoshidas found and remembered her two years later, who knew what lengths they'd go to in their pursuit of her? Whatever happened, she certainly did not want to end up married to someone she'd never met.

"I'm sorry, I just have to go," she said simply. "I must."

Her supervisor nodded, sighing. "I can easily get you transferred to the Red Cross Hospital. Will that be far enough, do you think?"

Mitsuko looked at her. Somehow, it seemed like she might possibly understand her situation. Mitsuko nodded gratefully. The Red Cross Hospital was on the other side of Kawasaki. "And please don't tell anyone where I've gone?"

Her supervisor nodded again, and Mitsuko smiled with gratitude.

Within one week, Mitsuko had begun her new job at the huge, modern Red Cross Hospital. She had changed rooming houses, too, just to be on the safe side, saying goodbye to her roommates. She told them she was transferring to another hospital in Tokyo, to be closer to home. She took the train to work every morning. It was redolent with the smell of the various pomades the men put in their hair, and the only sound was the rustling of the newspapers as the lucky few with seats tried to relax on their way to work.

In one way, the transfer was nice, because this new job paid more. She wasn't sure about the status of her family debt to the Ōtakes, but surely she had to be getting close to paying it off? She'd been working on it in one way or another for ten years, shouldering the burden on her own. She was twenty-five years old, and had never known a day that belonged only to herself. She must be getting a little closer to her little house with the window?

Maybe she could ask for an accounting? Perhaps this wouldn't be considered too impolite or forward, if she were careful in how she phrased it. She began working out the wording in her head, and composed a courteous letter to Mr. Ōtake that very night.

13

A SPOILED CHILD

Mitsuko while she was working in Kawasaki, 1942

Mitsuko hurried through the Kawasaki train station on her way home from work. It was 1941, and the debt was nearly paid. Tonight she would begin searching for her little house. The advertisement section of the newspaper was held crushed under her arm as she pushed through the throng of people. She had to meet her mother first, and give her this final allotment from her paycheck. The remainder would go to Ōtake-san, to be applied to the balance of the debt. Then she would be free to begin the search for her little house.

Tonight.

She felt a hand on her shoulder, and shook it off without turning around. There were rude, aggressive men everywhere in Japan these days, especially in the crowded train stations. They felt a kind of anonymity in being among such huge numbers of people, oddly free to do things they would never dream of doing in a one-on-one situation. She doggedly kept walking without turning around.

"Excuse me, but aren't you Nurse Ishikawa? Who used to work at Kawasaki Community Hospital?" a woman's voice asked.

Mitsuko turned around as she slowed, causing the homeward-bound people to part and go around her and the person whose hand was on her shoulder.

"My name is Yoshida," the woman was saying, nodding hello. "You probably don't remember me, but you took care of my daughter when she was hospitalized for tuberculosis two years ago at Kawasaki Community Hospital," the woman continued.

Mitsuko looked into the woman's eyes. Of course she remembered her. How could she forget the person, the reason she changed jobs, uprooted her entire life?

"Yes," she responded with a smile of recognition and surprise. "What a pleasure to see you again, Yoshida-san. How is your daughter?"

"She's fine, thanks to your wonderful care," Yoshida-san replied. "But I'm so glad I ran into you! I searched and searched for you back then. I wanted to arrange a meeting between you and my brother, do you recall? We were searching for a wife for him, and you seemed like such a perfect match." The woman looked into Mitsuko's eyes expectantly.

"I'm so sorry, it was very rude of me not to say goodbye before I transferred, but it was very sudden," Mitsuko explained, "and I'd been waiting for the paperwork for quite a long time." She nodded her head for emphasis.

"Well, what luck that I ran into you here!" Yoshida-san declared, clapping her hands together in delight.

"You mean you still haven't found a wife for your brother?" Mitsuko asked politely.

Yoshida-san shook her head. "There were two possibilities, but he turned them both down," she explained. "So this is so lucky."

"Do you know, I lost your card," Mitsuko said, looking at the large clock at the top of the steps. Her mother would be waiting already, she had to hurry. "If you could give me another, I'll contact you. It's just that I have to meet someone right now—"

"Oh, I'll just walk with you," Yoshida-san said agreeably, following her up the steps. "I'm finished with my shopping, so I have plenty of time." She fell into step next to Mitsuko.

"So, are you still a nurse?"

Mitsuko nodded.

"And where do you work now?"

"At the Red Cross Hospital," Mitsuko answered. She couldn't think of a reason not to answer.

The woman with her nodded. "That's a wonderful hospital, very prestigious."

Her words irritated Mitsuko. She wasn't a nurse for prestige, she did it because she loved the work.

"Everyone needs nursing care," was all she said. She was trying to think of some way to get rid of this woman, to keep from having to introduce her to her mother.

"Well, I'll say goodbye here, then."

She could see her mother sitting on the bench outside the department store where they usually met.

"Oh, is that right? Goodbye, then," Yoshida-san said unwillingly, bowing a farewell.

Mitsuko had just finished giving her mother the money when she heard a familiar voice.

"Ishikawa-san!"

No. It could not *be.*

"You were in such a hurry to go that you forgot to take my card," Yoshida-san exclaimed with a smile as she approached the two women.

"Mitsuko! Where are your manners? Introduce us!" her mother prodded, tugging on her daughter's sleeve.

"Pardon my manners," Mitsuko murmured. "This is Yoshida-san, whose daughter I cared for at Kawasaki Community Hospital a few years ago." She turned to her mother. "This is my mother."

"Your *mother!*" Yoshida-san gushed. "Well, this is a lucky day indeed!" She turned eagerly to Mitsuko's mother. "When I met your daughter in the hospital, I told her that she would make a wonderful wife for my brother, but she transferred to another hospital, poof, and disappeared, before we had a chance to arrange anything. I happened to run into her today, right here on the steps of the station."

Mitsuko's mother turned grim eyes on her daughter. "I see. And did you know about her kind offer before your transfer?"

Mitsuko looked at the ground. "She may have mentioned something," she admitted. "But in the excitement of hearing about my transfer, I stupidly forgot."

"Well, well, it's no matter now," Yoshida-san said, proffering her card in Mitsuko's direction. "My brother still has no wife, and I've found you again, so please contact me."

Mitsuko's mother took the card and spoke. "I'll talk to my forgetful daughter's father regarding this matter, and write to you very soon, you have my word." She gave her daughter one more look before bowing to Yoshida-san and taking her leave.

Mitsuko went back to her rooming house with a heavy heart, and no thoughts of looking for her little house anymore. She knew that something had been set in motion in Kawasaki Station, like tossing a stone in a pond, which would have ripples spreading in every direction, for a long time.

Sure enough, within a week, she had a telegram from her mother, with two terse words:

Come home.

By DAWN'S first light she was getting off the train at the modern station that had been built in the village. She began walking toward her childhood home. She paused once, to watch a hawk, out hunting for its breakfast. It drifted like a flake of ash across the pale sky, hovering for a moment before folding its wings and hurtling silently down to capture the tiny baby rabbit and flap away, clutching it in its pointed talons.

It was full morning by the time she reached the house. Brothers and sisters young enough to still be living at home had gathered outside the house to greet her. She nodded silently to them and entered.

Her father sat at the kitchen table, his empty rice bowl before him, drinking a cup of tea.

All around him, Mitsuko could see evidence of the prosperity she'd brought to her family with her steady income over the years. The house had glass windows now, instead of mere openings, and an actual wood floor instead of dirt; a glass-fronted cabinet stood against one wall to hold the family dishes and crockery, and she could smell that meat had been prepared recently.

"It's been a long time since I've seen you. I'm glad to see that you're still healthy." He nodded at the chair across from him, and Mitsuko sat.

"I've been corresponding with a man named Yoshida." He pulled a letter out of his sleeve. "He says you nursed his daughter in Kawasaki when she had tuberculosis two years ago. Do you know who he is?"

Mitsuko nodded and looked at the floor.

"He says that his wife spoke to you about a possible marriage to her brother. Is this true?"

Mitsuko didn't even nod this time, but continued to look at the floor. Her father brought his fist down on the table, rattling the crockery and making Mitsuko flinch. "Answer me!"

"Yes."

"And why wasn't I informed of this?" Her father glared at her. Over his shoulder Mitsuko could see her brothers and sisters crowding in the doorway.

"I didn't think she was serious."

"And who are you to decide if she's serious?" He spit on the floor. "Stupid girl," he muttered.

He turned to look at her. "This letter says that you changed hospitals to get away from her, that you ran away from her! Did you do that?" At her nod, he continued. "How could you do such a thing? What do you think they would think of a man who could raise such a child? You have made me and our family a laughingstock."

He waved the letter, which made a crackling sound, like hulled rice.

"Do you even know about these people? Did you bother

to find out, before you dashed away like an idiotic rabbit?" Without waiting for an answer, he continued. "You're twenty-five, do you know how lucky you are that someone wants you at such an age?"

Mitsuko felt her tears but refused to humiliate herself even further by wiping them away. She stared at her father.

"Well," he said. "I have made my decision. I will not punish you for your behavior. The main thing is that they still want you. You will go to their home with your mother. You will tell Yoshida-san and his wife that you will marry her brother—" he glanced down at the letter, "—Hanamura-san."

He looked across the table at her, and his voice softened, though not with kindness, Mitsuko could tell. "Since you were born, you have had opportunities to have a good life, a better life than I ever had. And yet you have persisted in trying to please only yourself." He shook his head. "I don't understand how I could have raised such a self-centered, spoiled child. You make me so ashamed."

Finally Mitsuko spoke, and she could not keep her voice from breaking. "What if he is unkind? What if I want to leave?"

Her mother shook her head in disbelief upon hearing her daughter's words.

Her father rose as if to go, but he addressed his last remarks to the wall above her head, not meeting her eyes. "Once you are married, your name will no longer be Ishikawa. You will no longer be my responsibility. If you insist on remaining as spoiled as you have been, if you decide to leave, it will be your husband's shame, not mine any longer." Her father turned and left the house.

Mitsuko put her head on her arms and wept, until her mother placed a hand on her shoulder. She looked up to see that her mother had set a piece of paper, an inkwell, and a brush pen in front of her. Mitsuko took a deep breath, wiped her tears with the heel of her hand, dipped the pen into the inkwell, and began to write:

Dear Yoshida-san,

Please forgive my untoward behavior toward your wife. I would be pleased to come to your home to meet your brother-in-law, and to discuss marriage...

14

A NEW BRIDE

Mitsuko and Tadaichi's wedding photo. 1942

Mitsuko looked around her new house. Of course, it wasn't "new," but it was new to her. It was on the outskirts of Kawasaki, an older dwelling, certainly built before the turn of the century. It had a small back room where her mother-in-law slept, and a main room where she slept with her new husband, Tadaichi-san. In addition to these rooms, there was a kitchen and a tiny formal room at the front of the house for entertaining.

Still, it was a step up for Mitsuko, and there was no question of her saying no to the offer of marriage. Tadaichi-san's sister, and even his *mother*, were educated women, both of whom could read, which was an amazing fact. Mitsuko had stared at her future mother-in-law with grudging respect.

She had seen the stack of newspapers next to the door, and the shelves of books, and her spirits rose. There would be something to read in this house, every day. There weren't many, but what books there were had shown signs of wear and of care.

And there was a *radio*.

As far as her new husband, there were things about him she found admirable, she supposed. He had a beautiful hand, she knew, though he'd never written her anything. There was something to be said for nice penmanship. Her awful calligraphy was one of the things she was most ashamed of, so she was proud she'd married someone who had such skill in that area.

And he was very musical. Music was something Mitsuko had no experience with, except the time she'd heard the *violin* in the train station. Tadaichi-san could play both the piano and the accordion, of all things; plus, he had a contraption set up on top of his accordion to which he'd attach a harmonica, and he could play that *at the same time*, something Mitsuko had never seen before.

He also liked to paint and spent hours in front of an easel, using his carefully hoarded oil paints to produce pictures of trees and rivers, Mt. Fuji, and places Mitsuko had never heard of, in a country called Europe.

So really, he was quite a cultured person, Mitsuko mused. If only being married to him weren't so *lonely*.

She supposed she was lucky that at least her mother-in-law, Yuki-san, had another place to sleep, so she was spared the embarrassment of having her nightly intimacies overheard. Obviously, as a well brought-up Japanese girl,

Mitsuko had gone to her wedding night a virgin, but as an experienced midwife she knew the rudiments of relations between a husband and a wife. She had been unprepared, however, for the discomfort of it, the messiness, the *bother*. She had barely spent two hours in Tadaichi-san's company before their wedding, and certainly no time alone. They had met in front of her parents and his mother, and his sister and her husband. There had been lots of bowing.

They were nice people, though they had come down a bit in the world. It was true that they did own land, but it was next to worthless, and they had spent nearly all the money they had just on getting Tadaichi-san set up with what he needed, clothing and equipment-wise, for his job at the military factory where he worked.

Today was Sunday, her day off from the hospital. She had been allowed to keep her job, which was a miracle of sorts. She was a nurse, and they were in the middle of a war, so circumstances warranted Mitsuko keeping her job, everyone agreed, even Tadaichi-san himself, though he hadn't looked happy about it. Mitsuko reflected that her life wasn't really much different from before, except that her money now went to her husband instead of to her father's creditor. She certainly never saw the money herself.

And Tadaichi-san was at work today, so she didn't have to think about what to say to him, which was a relief. It was funny, how she thought of him by his first name, but had yet to speak it out loud. Whenever she had to address him, she always called him *anata,* which was the honorific form of the pronoun "you."

So Mitsuko's life had settled into a new routine, of waking up early, preparing breakfast for the three of them, going to work, and coming home in the evening, usually to a meal prepared by her new *okasan,* Tadaichi-san's mother.

The three of them would sit together and eat, while she and Okasan talked about the day's events. Then the two of them would clean up together, and Mitsuko would read the smaller printed articles in the paper out loud, after which they would listen to her husband perform on the accordion and harmonica. They no longer owned a piano.

If not for the distasteful activities she had to perform in her futon at night, life would have been quite pleasant, Mitsuko reflected. And even those things were duties, she told herself. She had no choice in the matter. And it usually didn't take long, so at least there was that.

From left to right: Mitsuko's mother-in-law, her husband, Tadaichi-san (standing), and Mitsuko, ca 1942, shortly after their marriage. No one knows who the seated man in the middle is.

Sometimes, when she was cleaning on her days off, she would look out the tiny window of the front room of the house, the room that was hardly ever used, and think about the house that she'd planned to buy for herself. It was going to have a room like this, she remembered, with a table for one, where she'd keep a vase for flowers that she'd arrange herself. She'd taken a certificate in *ikebana* after all, and for what, if not to make beautiful arrangements of flowers, just like Hideko-san had done?

She also had a small bundle wrapped in a purple *furoshiki*, a traditional Japanese wrapping cloth, that sat in the little front closet next to the entrance of their house. Her mother-in-law had come across it once or twice, and pointed it out to Mitsuko.

"What is that?" she'd asked. "Is it yours?"

"Oh, that?" Mitsuko responded. "It's just something old of mine. It's nothing important, I just haven't put it away yet."

It contained a change of clothes and a little money, folded in some bills so it wouldn't clink together.

Sometimes, Tadaichi-san would go out at night and come home drunk. These times he would be rough and sloppy, and Mitsuko would try to turn away and pretend she was sleeping. He wouldn't care, though, and would want to do things anyway. If she resisted too much, he'd slap her, and tell her to "behave" or "be good, I'm almost finished." And finally, Mitsuko would have to just lie still and take it, and wait for him to be finished.

Tadaichi-san with his accordion, ca 1942

She didn't want to get pregnant, either, and tried to avoid those times of the month that she knew were risky, but she couldn't tell him that's what she was doing, because that would have made him angry, too. And she couldn't tell her mother-in-law that, either. For one thing, she wouldn't understand why. She was eagerly waiting for a grandchild, preferably a grandson. Every month, she would sigh when

Mitsuko hung up her special undergarments after washing them out.

Mitsuko and Tadaichi-san, ca 1942

"You're bleeding again?" she would ask, touching the underwear as Mitsuko hung them.

Mitsuko would merely nod as she clipped them to the line.

"Too bad," Okasan would say, shaking her head as she turned away. "Maybe next month."

And Mitsuko would feel bad, because her mother-in-law was a nice woman, a kind person, and she didn't deserve to be lied to.

She bided her time, trying to figure out the best time to run away, to make her escape. She also thought about where the best place would be to escape to, where no one would ask questions, where she could get a job as a nurse, maybe just tell everyone she was a sad war widow or something and just be alone.

Then, after she'd only been married for five months, she missed her period. She waited and waited, but her underwear remained clean and blameless, and she knew. Then, one night, she was carrying some boxes, and her breasts hurt where they pressed on her, and Okasan noticed.

She pressed on one of Mitsuko's breasts, grinning and cackling with glee when Mitsuko winced. "Finally!" she rejoiced. "Nearly half a year, but you're finally going to have a baby!" She quickly began retying her bun, then moved on to her sash. "I'd better get to the grocer's before they close, and see if they have any new rice so we can celebrate!" She grasped Mitsuko's arm, patting it after. "And I'll see if I have enough money to get some eggs for you, too."

Mitsuko nodded, trying to smile. Okasan was a good woman, a nice person. It wasn't her fault that her ungrateful and unworthy daughter-in-law didn't want to be here.

"If this is the first cycle you've missed, then the baby will be born in—let's see—February!" Okasan exclaimed. "And next year is the year of the rabbit! Not a good year for boys, but not terrible, either, so that's okay, that's okay. I can't wait to tell Tadaichi-san when he comes home tonight!"

Mitsuko had to smile at Okasan's joy. A new baby was a wonderful thing.

And she could probably raise one child on a nurse's salary, couldn't she?

15

A YOUNG MOTHER

Baby Haruko, wearing the red and black kimono Mitsuko made, 1943
The collar was added at the photographer's studio

The baby girl was born on February 10th, 1943. The labor was relatively short, and not very difficult, considering it was a first baby. Everyone said it was because Mitsuko was stout and had a large bottom, so she could really push.

She bowed to her mother-in-law as soon as she was able, to apologize for giving birth to a girl, though Okasan waved her words away.

"She is healthy, that's all that matters," Okasan consoled, patting her. "He might not say it, but Tadaichi-san won't mind, either. I know he will be happy with either a boy or a girl." He was off fighting the war, somewhere in the Pacific. He was supposed to come home on leave in a few days, when the baby was expected, but she had come a bit early.

Okasan picked up the bundle, holding the red-faced little one with the shock of black hair. "And look at how fat she is already!" she said with a smile. "So alert, and squalling before she was completely birthed."

Okasan looked at Mitsuko, who had lain back down already with a sigh. "You did a good job," she assured her daughter-in-law. "Your next one will be a boy, I'm sure."

Mitsuko just nodded and closed her eyes. "Easy" or not, she was exhausted.

She heard her baby cry and hoped she'd stop. She didn't have any milk for her yet, and she knew that nursing her wouldn't make her quiet for very long.

Sure enough, when her husband came home six days later, his face broke into a pleased smile to see the baby girl at her mother's breast. He named her Haruko, and gave Mitsuko some money to buy material for a new kimono for her. He even went with her to pick out the fabric.

Tadaichi-san and Mitsuko went to the shop together, leaving baby Haruko at home with his mother. It was Mitsuko's first time out with her husband, and she was a little startled at the change in him. He was jocular and personable, greeting everyone they met, explaining their errand to the shopkeeper.

He finally chose the fabric himself, settling on a red and black pattern with a green and purple floral motif. "This is good," he declared. "It's bright, with a hint of the spring that is to come." He turned to Mitsuko. "Don't you agree?"

Mitsuko looked at the fabric and considered. It wasn't a fabric she would've chosen herself, but it was nice, very bold and bright. It even had butterflies and birds on it. A baby wearing those colors would grow up friendly and confident, she believed. It seemed expensive to her, but Tadaichi-san waved away the cost. "It's for my firstborn child, my precious daughter," he said, waving away her concerns with a smile. "Don't worry about it."

So they bought the material, and Mitsuko worked on the kimono, finishing both it and the puffy overgarment, which needed cotton batting inside, in a couple of weeks. Even though it took a bit of time, she raised the stitching at the shoulders, so they could be lowered at a later date, and it could be worn after Haruko grew. She knew that Okasan would take the garment to be examined by the neighboring wives as well, so she did her best stitch work, taking her time and making them even.

She was pleased with the finished result, and knew that her mother-in-law was as well. Mitsuko smiled at her baby daughter as she passed her arms through the sleeves, though she was much too young to smile back.

Mitsuko had made a red obi as well, and she tied it around Haruko's waist. She picked the baby up when she was finished dressing her, enjoying how red her cheeks were.

"You're even fatter than when you were born, aren't you?" Mitsuko crooned.

Baby Haruko gurgled back at her, making Mitsuko smile once more.

"Mitsuko! Are you ready to go?" Okasan called as she emerged from the back bedroom. "The photographer won't want to be kept waiting, you know? Let's leave, shall we?"

Mitsuko nodded and rose, hoping her own kimono still fit well enough. She still hadn't lost all the weight she'd gained from her pregnancy, but Tadaichi-san's furlough was over in a couple of days, and he wanted a family photograph before he had to return to his post.

It had been a nice visit, at least in part because Mitsuko was still bleeding from giving birth to Haruko. Tadaichi-san knew this, and hadn't come near her at night, though usually it was a common event when he came home on his furloughs.

This visit, however, had just been filled with music, laughter, and fussing over the new baby. And her husband had even spoken to her and asked her opinion about things.

After he left, his sister, Chiyo-san, the one who'd introduced them, came to live with them, along with her daughter. Her husband was of course away fighting the Americans, like Tadaichi-san, and Chiyo-san didn't like living alone. Some of the shelling had come very near her home, too, and she was anxious.

So Mitsuko, who had actually almost started to feel settled in her new life, and had kind of begun to enjoy being mistress of the house, had to adjust to living with another woman and her daughter.

Chiyo-san believed that, since she was Mitsuko's elder, and Okasan was her actual mother, and the house where they all lived had actually been her house until her marriage, she was mistress of the house if anyone was.

"Mitsuko, you and Haruko are going to have to sleep in the other room with Okasan," Chiyo-san announced on the first day. "My daughter Sachiko and I will be sleeping in this room while we're living here."

Mitsuko looked at her sister-in-law in surprise. This was the biggest room in the house, and could easily accommodate three people and a baby. She looked at Okasan, to gauge her reaction. She merely kept sipping her tea and perusing the newspaper.

Apparently Mitsuko was on her own.

She nodded acquiescence and continued preparing the vegetables for dinner.

And there were more changes in store as well, it seemed.

They received much of their food via a co-op which delivered to a central location that rotated from week to week. When it was their turn to host, Mitsuko would lay it out in the entry of their house and let the neighborhood housewives know that the food had arrived. After they had come and made their selections, Mitsuko would take her household's portions. This was the accepted way of doing it, the way everyone did it.

The week after Chiyo-san and her daughter arrived, the co-op food delivery came to their house. Mitsuko came home from work, saw the order, and began to lay out the fish and other staples so the neighborhood could make their selections.

Chiyo-san drank tea and supervised, pointing out to Mitsuko the best way to lay everything out. Mitsuko tried to hurry and get everything done so she could nurse Haruko, who was minded by her mother-in-law during the day, and maybe spend a little time with her before dinner.

When Mitsuko was finished, Chiyo-san stepped forward and selected the biggest and best fish. It was obviously the freshest, as well. Its eye was round and shiny, and still popping out from the flesh, and its scales had an iridescent sheen to them.

Next, Chiyo-san chose the best, firmest tofu, and the hardest, newest apples.

Mitsuko bit her lip, but said nothing. She went to the street, called the neighbors, and went inside to reach eagerly for her daughter.

Haruko had lately learned to smile, and her red, wind-chapped cheeks would bunch up as her eyes nearly disap-peared when she saw her mother, making happy noises as she leaned toward her.

This was the best part of Mitsuko's day.

In July, Tadaichi-san came home for another furlough, and Mitsuko actually welcomed his return. They had Haruko in common, after all, Haruko, who was now a laugh-ing, bubbly, bright five-month-old baby with two little teeth in her mouth, and fine, black hair. She could even almost sit up all by herself.

Mitsuko smiled as she prepared dinner, watching Tadaichi-san play with their daughter.

During dinner, Tadaichi-san said, "This food is very good, so much better than what we get in the army."

"It should be," Mitsuko responded, laughing. "Chiyo-san picks the best for us instead of letting everyone else choose first, did you know?"

Sachiko stopped eating, chopsticks midair, her eyes moving from her uncle to her mother, who was staring at Mitsuko.

Mitsuko was eating while entertaining Haruko, who was lying in a home-made baby sling, made out of a sash that was tied to Mitsuko's body. Haruko lay across Mitsuko's front in the sling, diagonally, facing her mother.

Tadaichi-san got very still at his wife's words, then suddenly he flung his hot bowl of miso soup in her face. She gasped in shock and pain when the scalding liquid hit her, coating her head and shoulders.

She immediately checked the baby to make sure she was okay, and thankfully, she was.

"Be quiet," Tadaichi-san said in a low voice. "Chiyo is my sister, and you'll speak of her with respect, always. Understand?"

Mitsuko just nodded.

Sachiko's chopsticks continued their motion toward her rice bowl, and Chiyo-san smiled a small smile of triumph as she picked up her tea. Okasan didn't say a word, and continued chewing.

From her place at her mother's bosom, baby Haruko found a piece of tofu stuck to her mother's front and tried to poke at it with an uncoordinated, chubby finger.

Mitsuko wiped herself as best as she could and continued eating.

Tadaichi-san left for the front the following week, and three weeks later Mitsuko missed another period.

16

THE END OF A DREAM

Tomiko, wearing the same kimono, 1944

M itsuko's second pregnancy was more difficult to bear than the first had been, in more ways than one. She was tired, emotionally, spiritually, and physically. It was harder to get through the days. Taking care of Haruko meant she was already more exhausted than she had been during her first; just the physical act of carrying around a baby was fatiguing. She had two extra people to take care of at home, because of Chiyo-san and her daughter. Even though they were female, they weren't inclined to help very much, and Mitsuko was known for being a hard worker. And she was the *oyome-san*, the bride, it was her job, after all, to do most of the chores. Throw in the fact that the war wasn't going well, and that there weren't as many necessities to go around, and it was just a more difficult time, all the way around.

Haruko was her only joy. She lived for the moments they spent together. She loved the days she spent at home, washing and hanging clothes, Haruko strapped to her back; she loved singing to her, feeling her small hands playing with her hair. Day by day she felt her new baby, her new burden, growing large within her, and she knew that, as it grew, her dream of leaving this life, of taking Haruko and escaping, grew conversely smaller and dimmer.

Every time she got a new letter from Tadaichi-san, she'd add it to the stack of letters she kept with her stationery, her precious brush and ink and paper, and the few letters she'd managed to save from the omawarisan. She wondered where he was, and if he was safe.

The baby inside her fluttered to life as the winter came on, and the bombing over Kawasaki grew more and more frequent. The decision was made in February of 1944 that they would evacuate to the country, closer to Mount Fuji. She would have to leave her job at the hospital, but the train tracks leading to that part of town had been bombed to oblivion anyway, and she could no longer get there without risking a harrowing journey through burning rubble, so maybe it was for the best.

On a brutally cold day, Mitsuko, seven months pregnant, boarded a train with Haruko, Okasan, Chiyo-san and Sachiko and headed out of Kawasaki, leaving the bombed and burning city behind. The sky was the color of wet cement, and the air smelled of smoke and exhaust. Mitsuko spent most of the train ride feeling ill and sleeping, while

Okasan kept one-year-old Haruko on her lap and entertained her.

After nearly twelve hours on the train, which stopped and started for no discernible reason, they finally arrived at their destination, a nameless station in the middle of a rice field, literally, it seemed. Of course, it was bare at this time of year, just lonely squares of soil.

They found the one room dwelling they'd been assigned in the dark, and lit candles and the stove, rolling out pallets and settling down as best they could. Mitsuko nursed Haruko to sleep, wondering what life in this harsh, cold place would hold for them all.

By the light of day, things didn't look much better. It was one of a row of temporary dwellings, freezing cold now, that would obviously be terribly hot in the summer. There was one privy behind the house for the entire row of ten dwellings to share, and a creek nearby for washing.

Still, it did have a floor, and windows and a roof. They should be grateful, as Okasan said.

There was a meeting in the middle of the street later that morning, where they were told that Mitsuko and Chiyo-san would be working in the rice fields during the day. Sachiko would be allowed to attend school, and Okasan, because she was so old, would remain at home and mind Haruko, and the new baby, when it arrived.

After the meeting, as they were eating lunch in their one room home, Chiyo-san remarked, "So, after all of your education and training, you've wound up working in the rice fields after all, I guess. Hmm?"

Mitsuko didn't respond.

∾

THEY BEGAN WORKING the following week, preparing the
fields for the spring planting. It was backbreaking labor,
literally, with most of the time spent bent at the waist, facing
the paddy. No one cared that Mitsuko was pregnant; she
wasn't the only one, anyway. Sometimes she could hardly
straighten at the end of the day. And it only got worse when
the time came to plant the seedlings. They had to be pressed
into the water at exactly the right depth, exactly the right
distance apart.

The foreman did notice her, though. Most of the
workers were paid in rice, enough for two cooked bowls for
a day's work. They could not have survived without it, for
wartime rations were extremely skimpy by this time. He
would walk by the workers as they stood in front of the
paddies they'd planted, examine their work, and pour the
rice into bags that they held open as they waited.

After the second day, as the foreman examined
Mitsuko's work, he remarked to the person pulling the
wheelbarrow behind him that it was very good. "I can
always tell when this woman has been working on a paddy,"
he said. "Look how straight and even her seedlings are, as if
a machine has planted them." He nodded his approval, and
made a point of making sure everyone watched him pour
three cups of rice into her waiting sack.

Mitsuko bowed her thanks, making sure her head went
down very low, and that her forehead was parallel to the
ground. She and Chiyo-san had been sharing their portion
with Okasan so she could have something to eat, but today
they wouldn't have to.

That night, everyone got their own bowl of rice, and
even Chiyo-san was silenced as Mitsuko handed out the full
bowls and began feeding Haruko her dinner.

And the foreman paid Mitsuko an extra cup of rice every

day for as long as she worked in the paddies, for the remainder of the time they remained in the country near Mount Fuji.

Mitsuko went into labor in Late April, and gave birth to another girl after less than twelve hours. Since Tadaichi-san wouldn't be coming to visit, not even for a furlough, Okasan was given the privilege of naming the new baby. She decided to name her Tomiko. Mitsuko was glad, because she liked the name, and she knew that, even if she hadn't liked it, she wouldn't have been able to say anything anyway

Tomiko was a solemn baby from the beginning, very different from Haruko. Maybe she was aware that she'd come into the world under more harrowing circumstances, Mitsuko mused. She was a bit smaller than Haruko had been, a bit paler. Her eyes were rounder, not the classic, almond shape of most Japanese babies. Her hair, too, was a little bit brown, "chestnut," as Okasan said. This was considered a flaw in Japan.

"Do other people in your family have this color of hair?" Chiyo-san asked an exhausted Mitsuko as she examined the newborn.

Mitsuko just shook her head.

"Really?" Chiyo-san probed. "Because this isn't a family trait from our side. Everyone in my family has good, black hair, like Japanese people are supposed to have," she informed her sister-in-law.

Again, Mitsuko didn't respond, cuddling the baby close, as if she could shield her from her aunt's sharp words.

Mitsuko went back to the fields to work the following day, though she was allowed to take breaks from time to time to nurse the new baby, whom Okasan would bring out to the paddies.

The summer wore into the fall, and finally the rice ripened and was harvested, and Mitsuko could rest a little, though there was always something that needed to be done. The war was going very badly, and Tadaichi-san had been moved to the Chinese front, to Manchuria, where the fighting was more hand-to-hand combat, and very vicious. Letters couldn't get through, and they didn't even know if he was alive. Okasan spent some of their precious coins every month on incense to burn in his name, making sure it was read at the temple.

They spent most of that winter huddled around the stove, waiting for the periodic deliveries of food. Tomiko actually fared the best, because her diet consisted mainly of breast milk, and Mitsuko was still stout, with extra body fat, and had good, nutritious milk to offer her daughter.

Mitsuko worried endlessly about Haruko, who at nearly two was much too small, in her opinion. Even her red, chapped cheeks seemed to have shrunk. Mitsuko gave Haruko as much of her own share of the food as she could, only eating what she felt she needed to keep her milk supply healthy for Tomiko. Even Okasan gave extra vegetables to Mitsuko and Haruko, though Chiyo-san complained about this.

"Why don't you give anything extra to me?" she asked. "I'm your only daughter, and I'm hungry, too!" She was upset because she found out that Okasan had bartered some thread for two tangerines, and had given one each to Mitsuko and Haruko.

"Haruko is growing, and Mitsuko needs it for the baby," Okasan responded in a tired voice. "Can we stop talking and go to sleep?"

"What about Sachiko, then?" Chiyo-san continued. "She's growing, isn't she?"

"I don't mind," Sachiko spoke up in the dark. She was a good girl, and hated strife as well.

Chiyo-san voiced her displeasure one last time, and the dwelling was finally quiet.

THE COLD, wet spring finally arrived, and rice season with it, which was a blessing, because they would finally get their daily allotment of rice once more. The only problem was that, over the cold winter, Haruko had gotten used to having Mitsuko around all the time. She wasn't a baby any longer, but was rather a two-year-old toddler, alert and aware of her mother's comings and goings.

No matter how quiet Mitsuko tried to be when she left in the morning, Haruko would hear her and wake up. Mitsuko would be a few hundred yards down the road when she would hear Haruko's little voice, crying for her.

"*Okasan! Okasan! Ikanaide!* Mother! Don't go!" And Mitsuko would turn around to see her older daughter running down the dirt road in the early dawn, chasing after her as her mother-in-law trailed close behind.

As the weather warmed, the mosquitoes would swarm as the sun rose, and Haruko would be attacked by them the moment she stepped out of their little hut. This didn't deter her, however, and poor Mitsuko's heart broke as she hurried away from her child and her pitiful cries in the morning air, picturing her thin legs being bitten to bits by the blood-thirsty insects.

By the end of summer, Haruko had another fear in her two-and-a-half-year-old heart. The mother who lived next door to them had passed out in the heat and humidity of the rice paddy, and drowned in the shallow water, because no one had noticed. She became convinced that Mitsuko, too, would perish in such a manner, and simply slip away under the surface of the paddy.

"No, don't go don't go don't go," she would beg, clinging to Mitsuko's legs. This would wake baby Tomiko and make her cry as well, and Mitsuko's mother-in-law would have two crying babies to deal with when Mitsuko was finally able to get out of the house with Chiyo-san to work in the rice fields.

Then, on August 6th, the United States dropped an atomic bomb on Hiroshima, followed three days later by another on Nagasaki. Six days after that, the Emperor was on the radio, explaining to the people of Japan that the war was over, that they had to accept defeat, and somehow carry on living.

Mitsuko discovered that she didn't care at all about the fact that her country had been defeated. She only cared that she and her little girls had survived.

Within two weeks after that, they were given the all-clear to return to Kawasaki, and they'd also been informed that her husband had survived the war and would be returning from Manchuria by the end of October.

Mitsuko looked at her two sleeping babies on their last night in the one-room hut in the country, knowing that she would never leave this family, that the old woman who was snoring next to the window would be in her life until the day she died.

This was fine, because she was actually a very kind mother-in-law, a good woman, a nice person. And Chiyo-san and her daughter were returning to their home, which was another good thing. In addition, and in spite of every-thing, she knew that she owed it to this family to produce a son for them, and that it was probably even a good thing that her husband had survived so that this might happen also.

Mitsuko sighed and lay down between her daughters. The life she'd envisioned for herself once upon a time would never happen, she knew. But that didn't mean that a good life couldn't happen for her daughters.

She closed her eyes. Hopefully she could get some sleep before morning came.

EPILOGUE

Obachan with my daughter, 1997, at my house in California.
This was one of her favorite pictures because of the flowers.

My Obachan moved back to Kawasaki with her two daughters and her mother-in-law. Her husband returned to her from the Manchurian front, and two years later she gave birth to a boy, Takayuki, my uncle. By then, she had long since given up any idea of leaving, of course. The purple furoshiki had been unwrapped, the sparse belongings contained within it unpacked, the dreams it carried scattered to the wind.

They had been replaced by new dreams, maybe. Obachan always said she didn't mind staying with Ojichan because, no matter how much they disagreed about anything else, he did agree that education was everything, and he didn't mind spending money on the best schooling they could provide for their three children.

Haruko married a man who owned a futon shop, and had two children, a girl and a boy.

My mother married an American who was in the Navy and had a daughter. My uncle married a woman from the company where he worked and had three children, one of whom died as a teenager of muscular dystrophy. My obachan was so proud of all of us. All of her children finished college, as did all of their children, which was very important to her.

And my obachan did fulfill some of her own dreams as well. She became a teacher of ikebana. She was a midwife, a school nurse, and a teacher for nearly thirty years, capable, generous, and patient, the best obachan a granddaughter could ever hope to have. The house always seemed empty when she was gone, and one of the happiest sounds of my childhood was her voice calling out, "*Tadaimaa!*" after being gone all day. She always had a bag with her, and there always seemed to be something in it for me, no matter how long or how hard her day had been.

My obachan died in 2006, shortly after she told me the last bits of this story. I suppose if she'd lived, she might have told me more, though I don't know. The next part involves people who are still living, people who might object to seeing their lives in print. The truth is that the part of her story that I wanted to know, the part that involved her becoming the Obachan I knew, ended with the end of the war anyway. She put away her dreams of being alone, of being independent, of being a certain kind of person. She made a conscious decision to be someone else, a different kind of woman. She became the person I know, which is fine.

As for me, her second daughter's daughter, I am a writer of smexy romance novels, I love flowers very, very much, and I know what most of them are called in both English and Japanese, which I think would make her proud.

I loved my obachan with all my heart, and I miss her every day.

Obachan with one of her award winning flower arrangements, 1980s

MORE PHOTOS

Tadaichi (far right) with his work group, 1946

Tadaichi (my ojichan, or grandpa) and me, 1965

(Left to right) Yoriko, Tadaichi, Yuki (mother-in-law), Mitsuko, Haruko, and Takayuki, 1957